THE JOY LUCK CLUB

NOTES

including
- *Life and Background*
- *Introduction to the Novel*
- *List of Characters*
- *Critical Commentaries*
- *Genealogy*
- *Map*
- *Glossaries*
- *Critical Essays*
- *Review Questions and Essay Topics*
- *Selected Bibliography*

by
Laurie Neu Rozakis, Ph.D.
Associate Professor
SUNY College of Technology at Farmingdale

Wiley Publishing, Inc.

Editor
Gary Carey, M.A., University of Colorado

Consulting Editor
James L. Roberts, Ph.D., Department of English, University of Nebraska

Publisher's Acknowledgments
Reprint Editor: Michelle Hacker

Production
Wiley Publishing, Inc., Indianapolis Composition Services

CliffsNotes™ *The Joy Luck Club*

Published by:
Wiley Publishing, Inc.
111 River Street
Hoboken, NJ 07030
www.wiley.com

CONTENTS

Centerspread: Genealogy

THE JOY LUCK CLUB

Notes

LIFE AND BACKGROUND OF THE AUTHOR

Amy Tan, whose Chinese name, An-mei, means "blessing from America," was born in 1952 in Oakland, California, the middle child and only daughter of John and Daisy Tan, who came to America from China in the late 1940s. Besides Amy, the Tans also had two sons—Peter, born in 1950, and John, born in 1954.

The family moved nearly every year, living in Oakland, Fresno, Berkeley, and San Francisco before settling in Santa Clara, California. Although John and Daisy rarely socialized with their neighbors, Amy and her brothers ignored their parents' objections and tried hard to fit into American society. "They wanted us to have American circumstances and Chinese character," Tan said in an interview with Elaine Woo in the *Los Angeles Times* (March 12, 1989).

Young Amy was deeply unhappy with her Oriental appearance and heritage. She was the only Chinese girl in class from the third grade until she graduated from high school. She remembers trying to belong and feeling frustrated and isolated. "I felt ashamed of being different and ashamed of feeling that way," she remarked in a *Los Angeles Times* interview. In fact, she was so determined to look like an American girl that she even slept with a clothespin on her nose, hoping to slim its Asian shape. By the time Amy was a teen-ager, she had rejected everything Chinese. She even felt ashamed of eating "horrible" five-course Chinese meals and decided that she would grow up to look more American if she ate more "American" foods. "There is this myth," she said, "that America is a melting pot, but what happens in assimilation is that we end up deliberately choosing the American things—hot dogs and apple pie—and ignoring the Chinese offerings." (*Newsweek*, April 17, 1989)

Amy's parents had high expectations for her success. They

decided that she would be a full-time neurosurgeon and part-time concert pianist. But they had not reckoned with her rebellious streak. Ever since she won an essay contest when she was eight years old, Amy dreamed of writing novels and short stories. Her dream seemed unlikely to become reality, however, after a series of tragedies shook her life. When Amy was fifteen years old, her older brother Peter and her father each died of brain tumors within the same year. Deciding that the remaining family needed to escape from the site of their tragedy, Daisy settled with Amy and her brother in Montreux, Switzerland.

The move intensified Amy's rebellion. "I did a bunch of crazy things," she told Elaine Woo. "I just kind of went to pieces." Perhaps the most dangerous was her relationship with an older German man who had close contacts with drug dealers and organized crime. Daisy had the man arrested for drug possession and got her daughter hauled before the authorities. Amy quickly severed all ties with the German.

A year later, Daisy, Amy, and John returned to San Francisco. In 1969, Amy enrolled in Linfield College, a small Baptist university in McMinnville, Oregon. Daisy selected the college because she believed it to be a safe haven for her daughter. A year later, however, Amy followed Louis DeMattei, her Italian-American boyfriend, to San Jose City College in California. Just as distressing to Daisy, Amy changed her major from pre-med to English and linguistics. Daisy was so upset that she and her daughter did not speak to each other for six months.

Amy then transferred to San Jose State University and earned a B.A. in English and an M.A. in linguistics. After completing her degrees, Amy married DeMattei, a tax attorney. Still not certain what path to pursue, she entered a doctoral program in linguistics at the University of California at Santa Cruz and at Berkeley, but left in 1976 to become a language-development consultant for the Alameda County Association for Retarded Citizens. It was not until the early 1980s that she became a business writer.

As with all fairy tales, *The Joy Luck Club* had an unlikely beginning. Tan's business writing venture was so successful that she was able to buy her mother a house. Yet, despite her happiness at being able to provide for her mother, she was not fulfilled in her work. "I measured my success by how many clients I had and how many billable hours I had," she told interviewer Jonathan Mandell. Secretly, Tan had always wanted to write fiction, but she had thrown herself so completely into her freelance career that she spent more than ninety hours a week at it. Early in 1985, Tan began to worry that she was devoting too much time to her business and started looking for a change. She decided to force herself to do another kind of writing. The turning point came a year later, when Tan's mother was hospitalized after a heart attack. "I decided that if my mother was okay, I'd get to know her. I'd take her to China, and I'd write a book." Her only previous forays into fiction were "vacation letters written to friends in which I tried to create little stories based on things that happened while I was away," she noted.

The same year, Tan wrote a short story, "Endgame," about a brilliant young chess champion who has a difficult relationship with her overprotective Chinese mother. Tan expanded the story into a collection, and it was sold to the prestigious publisher G.P. Putnam. Because of her huge advance—$50,000—Tan dissolved her freelance business and completed the volume, which she named *The Joy Luck Club*. "I wrote it very quickly because I was afraid this chance would just slip out of my hands," she told Elaine Woo. She completed the manuscript in May 1988, and the book was published the following year. The book was greeted with almost universal acclaim. "Magical," said fellow novelist Louise Erdrich; " . . . intensely poetic and moving," echoed *Publishers Weekly*. "She has written a jewel of a book," Orville Schell concluded in the *New York Times* (March 19, 1989).

In April 1989, *The Joy Luck Club* made the *New York Times'* best-seller list, where it remained for seven months. Tan was named a finalist for the National Book Award for fiction and National Book Critics Circle Award. She received the Bay Area Book Reviewers Award for fiction and the Commonwealth Club Gold Award. Paperback rights for the novel sold for more than $1.23 million, and it has been translated into seventeen languages, including Chinese.

The phenomenal success of *The Joy Luck Club* and the unfamiliar rituals of being a celebrity made it difficult for Tan to concentrate on writing her second novel. At one time, writing it became such a challenge that she broke out in hives. She began seven different novels until she hit upon a solution: "When my mother read *The Joy Luck Club*," Tan said, "she was always complaining to me how she had to tell her friends that, no, she was not the mother or any of the mothers in the book . . . So she came to me one day and she said, 'Next book, tell my true story.'"

The Kitchen God's Wife, published in 1991, tells the story of Daisy's life through the fictional Winnie, a refugee from China. The book was a huge success even before publication: in a tightly fought contest, the Literary Guild bought the book club rights for a reported $425,000. Five foreign publishers bought rights to the novel—all before publication. In 1992, Tan published a children's book, *The Moon Lady*. The plot is taken from the "Moon Lady" episode in *The Joy Luck Club*. "The haunting tale that unfolds is worthy of retelling," *Publishers Weekly* wrote. When not writing, Tan enjoys playing pool. She is a frequent visitor to Family Billiards in San Francisco, the city where she and husband Louis DeMattei live.

A NOTE ABOUT MODERN ASIAN–AMERICAN LITERATURE

It was not until the 1976 publication of Maxine Hong Kingston's mystical memoir of her San Francisco childhood, *The Woman Warrior*, that Asian-American writers broke into mainstream American literature. Even so, ten more years had to pass until another Asian-American writer achieved fame and fortune. *The Joy Luck Club*, Amy Tan's first novel, sold an astonishing 275,000 hard-cover copies upon its 1989 publication. The success of Tan's book increased publishers' willingness to gamble on first books by Asian-American writers. Two years later, at least four other Chinese-American writers had brisk-selling books. Gus Lee's *China Boy*, for example, had an initial print run of 75,000, huge for a first-time author. His advance was nearly $100,000. The Literary Guild purchased the rights to the book; Random House did an audio version with *M. Butterfly's* B. D. Hong as the reader. Two publishers fought for the right to publish David Wong Louie's *Pang of Love*, a collection of short stories. Gish Jen's *Typical American* is an equally big hit.

At the same time, Japanese-American writers are flourishing. Perhaps not since the literary community "discovered" Jewish-American writers in the 1950s have we experienced such a concentrated ethnic wave. In part, this interest in Asian-American literature can be attributed to the near doubling of America's

Asian-American population, from 3.5 million to 6.9 million in the past ten years. The fact remains, however, that more Asian-Americans are writing, and their books have a fresh and original voice.

INTRODUCTION TO THE NOVEL

The Joy Luck Club describes the lives of four Asian women who fled China in the 1940s and their four very Americanized daughters. The novel focuses on Jing-mei (June) Woo, a thirty-six-year-old daughter, who, after her mother's death, takes her place at the meetings of a social group called the Joy Luck Club. As its members play mah jong and feast on Chinese delicacies, the older women spin stories about the past and lament the barriers that exist between their daughters and themselves. Through their stories, Jing-mei comes to appreciate the richness of her heritage.

Suyuan Woo, the founder of the Joy Luck Club, barely escaped war-torn China with her life, and was forced to leave her twin infant daughters behind. Her American-born daughter, Jing-mei "June" Woo, works as a copywriter for a small advertising firm. She lacks her mother's drive and self-confidence, but finds her identity after her mother's death, when she meets her twin half-sisters in China.

An-mei Hsu grew up in the home of the wealthy merchant Wu Tsing. She was without status because her mother was only the fourth wife. After her mother's suicide, An-mei came to America, married, and had seven children. Like Jing-mei Woo, An-mei's daughter Rose is unsure of herself. She is nearly prostrate with grief when her husband, Ted, demands a divorce. After a breakdown, she finds her identity and learns to assert herself.

Lindo Jong was betrothed at infancy to another baby, Tyan-yu. They married as preteens and lived in Tyan-yu's home. There, Lindo was treated like a servant. She cleverly tricked the family, however, and gained her freedom. She came to America, got a job in a fortune cookie factory, met and married Tin Jong. Her daughter, Waverly, was a chess prodigy who became a successful tax accountant.

Ying-ying St. Clair grew up a wild, rebellious girl in a wealthy family. After she married, her husband deserted her, and Ying-ying had an abortion and lived in poverty for a decade. Then she married Clifford St. Clair and emigrated to America. Her daughter, Lena, is on the verge of a divorce from her architect husband, Harold

Livotny. She established him in business and resents their unequal division of finances.

LIST OF CHARACTERS

The Mothers

Suyuan Woo

The central event in Suyuan's life is the loss of her twin baby daughters. In a desperate attempt to save her babies from the Japanese troops advancing through China, Suyuan leaves them by the side of the road. Soon after, she meets her second husband, Canning Woo. They emigrate to America and have a daughter. A strong, resourceful woman, Suyuan never gives up the search for her first two daughters.

An-mei Hsu

An-mei's mother, the wife of a respected scholar, loses all status when her husband dies; she is raped and forced into concubinage by the wealthy Wu Tsing. She kills herself so that An-mei can have freedom. An-mei comes to America, marries, and has seven children. Her youngest child, Bing, drowns in the ocean.

Lindo Jong

Betrothed at infancy to Tyan-yu, Lindo marries him when she is twelve years old, after floods destroy her parents' home. She is treated very badly and finally tricks the family into releasing her from the marriage. She comes to America, gets a job in a fortune cookie factory, meets and marries Tin Jong. They have three children: Winston, Vincent, and Waverly.

Ying-ying St. Clair

Ying-ying grew up a fearless, reckless girl amid great wealth. When her husband leaves her for an opera singer, she has an abortion and lives in poverty for ten years. Then she moves to the city and becomes a shop girl. She meets Clifford St. Clair, and they marry and move to America. He adores her, but she has lost her spirit. She must confront her past in order to regain her sense of self.

The Daughters

Jing-mei "June" Woo

Her mother tries to make her a piano prodigy, but Jing-mei lacks both talent and drive. Now a copywriter for a small advertising firm, Jing-mei is easily humiliated by those who possess greater self-confidence. She finds her identity when she meets her twin half-sisters in China, after her mother's death.

Rose Hsu Jordan

A timid person, Rose is unable to make decisions. Her husband, Ted, leaves her and demands possession of their home. After a breakdown, she comes into her own and learns to assert herself.

Waverly Jong

A childhood chess prodigy, Waverly becomes a successful tax accountant. After the failure of her first marriage, she falls in love with fellow accountant Rich Shields. She has a daughter, Shoshana, from her first marriage.

Lena St. Clair

Lena establishes her husband, Harold Livotny, in his own architectural firm, providing him with seed money and ideas. Eight years later, they are dividing the household expenses equally, although Harold now earns seven times more than Lena does. She is resentful and angry.

Minor Characters

Arnold

A neighborhood boy who teases Lena when they are children, he later dies of measles; Lena feels guilty, linking his death to her unwillingness to finish her daily rice. She develops an eating disorder.

Ted Jordan

Rose Hsu Jordan's husband; a physician; he sues Rose for divorce ostensibly because of her inability to make decisions. In reality, he is having an affair with another woman.

Tin Jong

Lindo Jong's husband; Waverly Jong's father.

Harold Livotny

Lena's husband; an architect.

Clifford St. Clair

Ying-ying's husband; Lena's father. A well-meaning man, he nonetheless cannot understand his wife's loneliness and isolation.

Wu Tsing

The wealthy merchant who forces An-mei Hsu's mother into concubinage by raping her.

Popo

An-mei's grandmother. She throws her daughter out of the house because of the disgrace that she brings upon the family.

CRITICAL COMMENTARIES

Part I: Feathers from a Thousand *Li* Away

A brief parable introduces one of the novel's primary themes: transformation. An old woman remembers purchasing an unusual "swan" in a Shanghai market; the swan had originally been a duck, but it stretched its neck so long—trying to become a goose—that it eventually looked exactly like a swan. The old woman took her swan and booked passage on a ship bound for America, and during the journey, she imagined what it would be like to raise a daughter in America. She hoped that her daughter would be valued for herself—and not valued as only a reflection of her husband. She would give her daughter this swan, "a creature that became more than what was hoped for."

In America, immigration officials immediately confiscated the swan and, in her confusion with all of the official forms and papers to fill out, the woman forgot why she came to America and what she left behind. Many years later, the woman still treasured a single feather from the wondrous swan; she planned to give her daughter this feather—she would do so on the day when she could speak "perfect American English" to her daughter.

Within this parable lies Tan's ironic treatment of the theme of the American Dream—the belief that America is a guaranteed Land of Opportunity, of success and happiness. An old woman sets off on a journey, certain that this fabled destination will ensure her a fresh start, a place where her daughter can gain respect and accomplish wondrous things, unburdened by the enormous hardships that she herself suffered in the past. In a sense, the woman's dream comes true: her daughter gains respect, but meantime, she becomes so Americanized—"speaking only English and swallowing more Coca-Cola than sorrow"—that the two women are unable to communicate with one another.

Inability to communicate because of the generation gap is yet another theme in this novel. On a literal level, the daughter can speak very little Chinese, and her mother's English is poor. On a figurative level, the daughter grows up without anguish or sorrow, so she cannot understand her mother's painfully tragic past, and her mother knows no way that she can communicate the depths and the details of her suffering to her sheltered, fortunate daughter. This mother-daughter tension is a key to understanding the lives of the four Chinese mothers and their American daughters, who are the central characters in this novel. Using this tension, Tan explores and reveals the emotional upheaval that results when people's hopes and expectations are continually thwarted by the realities of their lives.

This prologue, set in *italics*, introduces several of Tan's literary techniques. Notice, for example, how she constructs her novel by using parallelisms—the repetition of similar elements. Each of the four sections of the novel begins with a brief parable, set in italics. In addition, each section contains four separate stories, each of which will parallel one another in various ways.

Tan also uses symbolism—a person, place, or object that stands for, or represents, something beyond itself, such as an abstract idea or feeling. Initially, Tan uses the swan in its traditional fairy-tale sense to symbolize transformation. As the ugly ducking of the fairy tale matured into a beautiful swan, so the old woman who was degraded by her husband in China hopes that she will be transformed in American into her own person, someone whom her daughter can respect. More important, however, the woman hopes that her daughter will transcend this possibility of gaining respect and be transformed into "a creature that became more than what was hoped for."

Tan now creates her own fairy tale of the duck's becoming a swan. In her version, the duck initially hoped to become a magnificent goose, one that would someday be the centerpiece for a roast goose dinner. Ironically, the duck stretched its neck so long that it resembled more than it hoped for: it resembled a swan. Similarly, the old woman hopes that her daughter will become transformed in America. Ironically, the daughter is transformed—but she is transformed into an Americanized Chinese-American woman, one with whom her mother can no longer communicate. Like the duck, the daughter becomes so changed that her life is forever altered. The swan can never become a duck again; likewise, the daughter of the Chinese immigrant can never again be Chinese—only American. The swan has vanished and its single, remaining feather symbolizes a mother's almost extinguished expectations, the sparse remnants of her hopes and plans to bequeath her fierce optimism and rich Oriental heritage to her daughter.

As with most parables, there is a lesson here: Be careful what you dream. Your dreams may become reality—and more.

Jing-mei Woo: *The Joy Luck Club*

"Before I wrote *The Joy Luck Club*," Tan said in an interview, "my mother told me, 'I might die soon. And if I die, what will you remember?'" Tan's answer appears on the book's dedication page, emphasizing the novel's adherence to truth. How much of the story is real? "All the daughters are fractured bits of me," Tan said in a *Cosmopolitan* interview. Further, Tan has said that the members of the club represent "different aspects of my mother."

When the novel opens, a mother, Suyuan Woo, has died of a cerebral aneurysm, and her husband has asked their thirty-six-year-old daughter, Jing-mei ("June"), to assume her mother's role and take her seat at the next meeting of the Joy Luck Club. Suyuan innovated this particular version of the club long ago—in 1949, the year she arrived in San Francisco from China. At the First Chinese Baptist Church, she met the Hsus, the Jongs, and the St. Clairs, and soon she enticed the wives to join with her and form a Joy Luck Club.

In a flashback, we hear Suyuan telling her daughter about the origins of the very first Joy Luck Club, as well as stories from her past. Her first husband, an officer with the Kuomintang, feared an imminent Japanese invasion, so he took her and their two small babies to Kweilin. There, Suyuan created the Joy Luck Club in order to cope with the horrors of war. Each week, four young women met to play mah jong, share a few meager luxuries, and talk about happier times. Because Suyuan's stories about that first Joy Luck Club—especially the endings—change each time she tells them, June discounts them as little more than embroidered, restyled, improvised memories.

One day, however, Suyuan tells her daughter an entirely new story: an army officer arrived at their house in Kweilin and urged Suyuan to escape to Chungking as quickly as possible. The exodus was so effected suddenly and was so grueling that, along the way, she was forced to abandon all her possessions, one by one. Finally, she had to abandon her most precious possessions of all: her two baby daughters. June is stunned. She has two sisters, about whom she knew nothing—until now.

This central episode in this section of the novel is based on truth. In 1967, Tan, her mother Daisy, and her brother John left California for Switzerland. On the eve of their departure, Daisy revealed that somewhere in China, she had three daughters from an earlier marriage—daughters lost to her when political ties were severed between the U.S. and China in 1949. In the novel, Suyuan loses two daughters and does not live long enough to be reunited with them. In real life, however, Tan's mother, Daisy, was reunited with two of her daughters in 1978. Thus, Tan interweaves fact and fiction in the novel, taking truth from her mother's stories while creating a larger canvas for her novel, focusing on two cultures and two generations and the chasm between them. The transformation of truth into dramatic fiction parallels the transformation within each of the four mothers—from being young girls to being old women. The novel also focuses on the transformation of the Chinese daughters into full-fledged Americans. And, of course, Tan's emphasis on communication—and particularly the lack of communication—between the two generations is always present.

The novel, in fact, opens with the concept of communication: Mr. Woo, June's father, believes that his wife died because she could not express herself. Unvoiced ideas, he says, can literally cause death. A few paragraphs farther on, June alludes to the problems that she and her mother had communicating: "I can never remember things I didn't understand in the first place."

In "Mother Tongue," an essay in *The Threepenny Review*, Fall 1990, Tan commented on her problems communicating with her mother. "I think my mother's English almost had an effect on limiting my possibilities in life . . . While my English skills were never judged as poor, compared to math, English could not be my strong suit . . . for me, at least, the answers on English tests were always a judgment call, a matter of opinion and personal experience."

Tan is too modest. Her novel is rich—especially in figurative language, words and phrases that convey ideas beyond their literal meaning. Tan's most common figures of speech are similes, metaphors, personification, and hyperbole. Many critics have compared her narrative style and her unique voice to the Native American writer Louise Erdrich. Tan recalls reading Erdrich's *Love Medicine* in 1985 and being "so amazed by her voice. It was different and yet it seemed I could identify with the powerful images, the beautiful language and such moving stories." Tan's images are equally powerful. Her metaphor "the peaks looked like giant fried fish trying to jump out of a vat of oil," for example, uses a common food item eaten regularly within a terrifying context in order to convey the horrors of war and to foreshadow the unbearable events that will befall the mother who is forced to abandon her babies by the side of the road.

This section also introduces the theme of identity and heritage. June is ashamed of her heritage, symbolized by the strange clothes that the mothers wear to the Joy Luck Club; June is uncomfortable looking at the "funny Chinese dresses with stiff stand-up collars and blooming branches of embroidered silk sewn over their breasts." She imagines that the Joy Luck Club is a "shameful Chinese custom, like the secret gathering of the Ku Klux Klan or the tom-tom dances of TV Indians preparing for war." However, when June accepts the Joy Luck Club's gift of $1200, she takes a first step toward fully discovering, accepting, and appreciating her Oriental heritage.

Interestingly, Tan herself and her friends have formed their own version of the Joy Luck Club. They call it "A Fool and His Money" and use the club as a forum where they can exchange investment tips.

(Here and in the following sections, difficult words and phrases are translated for you, as are those below.)

- **she died just like a rabbit** Suyuan's stroke occurred in her brain, killing her instantly, just as one would club a rabbit in the head—without warning. She had no symptoms. One moment she was alive; the next, she was dead.

- **her first marriage . . . before the Japanese came** As early as 1920, Japan tried to conquer China. On September 18, 1931, they seized all of Manchuria. The following spring, they set up a puppet government, Manchukuo. In 1937, Japan and China plunged into full-scale war.

- **the Kuomintang** From 1928 to 1949, the Kuomintang was the main political party of China; founded by Sun Yat-sen in 1911 and later, led by General Chiang Kai-shek, it has been the main political party of Taiwan since 1949.

- **mah jong** an ancient Chinese game introduced to America in 1920. The game is played with dice, racks, and 144 domino-like tiles, divided into seven suits—bamboos (bams), circles (dots), characters (cracks), dragons, winds, seasons, and flowers. The game is usually played by four people. After the tiles are mixed, each player builds a wall two tiles high and about seventeen tiles long. The walls are pushed together to form a square. Players take tiles from the square to form specific combinations.

An-mei Hsu: *Scar*

To June Woo, the mothers who treasure the evenings that they spend together at the Joy Luck Club seem little more than elderly, middle-class women in their "slacks, bright print blouses, and different versions of sturdy walking shoes." Yet we know now that the life of June's mother, Suyuan, was repeatedly torn by tragedy. In a similar fashion, this chapter illustrates that the same is true of An-mei, the woman who sits in the south corner of the mah jong game, the woman characterized by June Woo as a "short bent woman in her seventies, with a heavy bosom and thin, shapeless legs." An-mei suffered tragedies of her own, just as did her own mother.

In a flashback to An-mei's childhood, we see that An-mei's mother was not the "fallen woman" that people told little An-mei that she was. Rather than being cold and uncaring, she deeply loved her small daughter—despite the fact that she abandoned An-mei, and the little girl had to be raised by her grandmother, Popo, her younger brother, and her uncle and aunt in their large, cold house in Ningpo.

In the flashback, An-mei's father is dead, and Popo wants An-mei to also think of her mother as dead because she brought great disgrace to the family by becoming a number-three concubine. It is clear that Popo loves her granddaughter, but she doesn't realize that her scary stories about children who do not obey adult authority frighten little An-mei and her brother.

For example, to protect her grandchildren from evil spirits, Popo tells them that they came from unwanted eggs of a stupid goose; they came from eggs so valueless that they weren't fit to be "cracked over rice porridge." An-mei believes this tale—literally; later, when her mother arrives unexpectedly, An-mei notes that her mother has a long neck "just like the goose that had laid me." Here, Tan extends her original parable of the duck who became more; An-mei's long-necked, goose-like mother transformed herself into something quite different—something entirely inappropriate, according to Grandmother Popo.

To An-mei, her mother looks strange, "like the missionary ladies." Her face is a dark shadow when An-mei first sees her; she seems insolent and bossy, and her foreign clothes and high-heeled shoes suggest evil, suggest a woman worthy of contempt—exactly as Popo and Auntie described her in their many tales about her to An-mei. However, the woman's tenderness toward little An-mei and her uncontrolled wailing at the memory of An-mei's being accidentally burned belie her Western—thus, suspect—appearance.

Tan's tapestry of narrative again unfolds yet another picture of uncomfortable identity and traditions of heritage. To honor Popo in the ancient, accepted way, in an attempt to save her from dying, An-mei's mother makes a physical sacrifice. Communication has been severed between An-mei's mother and Popo just as it was between June Woo and her mother. Now, An-mei's mother severs part of her own flesh to enrich the soup that she hopes will heal Popo.

In this scene, An-mei realizes that if one is to discover one's identity, one's heritage, one must metaphorically "peel off your skin, and that of your mother, and her mother before her. Until then, there is nothing." Nothing—that is—except the scar. An-mei herself bears a scar, a reminder of the day that her mother came to Popo's house and cried out, begging An-mei to come with her. Popo had damned her own daughter—and at that moment, a pot of dark boiling soup spilled on tiny An-mei.

The little girl almost died; she would have, in fact, if Popo hadn't revealed the love that she carried in her heart—but could not demonstrate—for An-mei's mother. Gently, she warned An-mei that if she did not get well, her mother would forget her. An-mei immediately began her recovery. Each of the daughters in this novel will, in individual ways, undergo this process of healing the divisiveness that separates them from their mothers.

Tan's figurative language and imagery reinforce the magical, fairy tale atmosphere that is threaded throughout the narrative. The images create an enchanted mood, where all sorts of strange things seem possible. This section opens with the image of An-mei's mother as a ghost. Popo tells the children about ghosts that steal strong-willed little girls. Later, An-mei's mother seems "to float back and forth like a ghost." Accordingly, in this fairy tale world, it shocks Western readers initially when An-mei's mother slices a piece of her own flesh into a pot of soup—and yet, it seems appropriate if she is to successfully create a healing charm. The child understands the meaning of this sacrifice.

- **So you see, to Popo we were also very precious** People from non-Western cultures often refuse to praise their children for fear that a vengeful god will seek retribution. They also follow specific rituals in order to ensure their children's safety from such spirits. Some Italian people, for example, wear charms to ward off evil spirits; some Jewish people hang a red ribbon on a baby's crib to protect the child from harm.

- **number-three concubine** Polygamy is a form of marriage in which a person has more than one mate. Polygamy has been widely practiced at various times by many people throughout the world, but has never been the norm. Usually only rich and powerful men have more than one wife. Polygamy sometimes results in the maintenance of separate households for each wife, as in some wealthy, pre-revolutionary Chinese families. The shared household was more frequent—especially with Muslims and many Native American tribes before the colonization of America. Polygamy is still common in some Muslim countries and in parts of Africa, but the practice is illegal in most of the world. Concubinage is a form of polygamy. The concubine's status is inferior to that of the primary wife. Her status declines the further removed she is from the primary wife. A number-three concubine, therefore, would have almost no status at all within the household. This practice was legal at one time in many countries, including pre-revolutionary China.

Lindo Jong: *The Red Candle*

Like earlier chapters, this one also deals with the theme of sacrifice and filial obligations. Earlier, An-mei's mother sacrificially mutilated herself for her mother; here, Lindo submits her life to her parents' plans for her future: "I once sacrificed my life to keep my parents' promise," the chapter begins. Lindo is willing to endure a carping, loveless marriage in order to ensure her parents' honor and prevent them from losing face. Only when she can escape with honor does she leave the doomed relationship with her husband.

Lindo explains that she was betrothed when she was only two years old—to a boy only a year old. By this time, people in cities were already making matches based on love, but Lindo's family was from the country and followed the old ways. When Lindo was twelve years old, the Fen River flooded the plains, ravaging the wheat crop, wrecking the land, and destroying their home. Since there was no insurance in those days, Lindo's family was suddenly penniless. Her father moved all the family members—except Lindo—to Wushi, a town near Shanghai. Lindo stayed behind to live with her future in-laws, the Huangs.

When Lindo arrived at the Huangs' home, she was in awe of the magnificence of their mansion; immediately, she sensed that they were wealthier than her family and that they looked down on her. The Huangs' house, however, was imposing only from the outside; inside, it was unadorned and uncomfortable, with barely enough room for all twenty relatives. There was no celebration when Lindo arrived; she was immediately shown to the servants' quarters.

Determined to honor her parents and prevent them from losing face, Lindo spent the next few years working hard—learning how to cook, sew, and clean—because she had promised her parents that she would be a good wife.

Lindo's monologue to her daughter reinforces Tan's theme of the generation gap. To Lindo and to Chinese women of her generation, it was accepted without question that children would sacrifice everything for their parents' wishes. To the Chinese-American children of today's generation, however, promises and sacrifices have little meaning: Lindo's daughter cannot even honor a simple promise to come to dinner. The girl can offer only feeble excuses. When she was a girl, Lindo had no choice. She had to obey.

Very quickly, Lindo discerned that her future husband, Tyan-yu, was arrogant and spoiled and that her future mother-in-law, Huang Taitai, was cruel and detached. When Lindo turned sixteen, Huang Taitai set the date for the upcoming marriage, planning an elaborate celebration. The Japanese invasion, however, kept nearly all the guests away.

So distraught that she wanted to throw herself into the Fen River, Lindo looked into the mirror and suddenly realized that even though Tyan-yu might own her body, he could never possess her soul. That night, the marriage was not consummated. Tyan-yu fell asleep, and Lindo blew out his end of the tradition-old marriage candle, which was lighted at both ends.

Months passed and Tyan-yu still wouldn't touch Lindo. Relieved, she came to love him like a brother, but he turned against her and lied to his mother, blaming Lindo for their lack of children. Huang Taitai confined Lindo to bed, took away all her jewelry, but still Lindo bore no children. By chance, noticing that a servant girl was pregnant by her boyfriend, Lindo devised a plan to make the Huangs think it was their idea to end the marriage. She awakened the entire house, screaming that in a dream, she saw the wind blow out Tyan-yu's end of the marriage candle: their marriage was doomed. Furthermore, in her dream she saw that Tyan-yu had impregnated a servant girl and, moreover, that the girl had imperial blood.

Lindo was granted a divorce, Tyan-yu married the servant girl, and Lindo traveled to America. Now, every few years when she has extra money, Lindo buys herself yet another twenty-four-carat gold bracelet, and once a year, she takes off all her gold and thinks about the day that she realized that she could be true to herself—as true and pure as twenty-four-carat gold.

The imagery of gold, which opened this section, ends this section, underscoring Tan's theme of faithfulness to one's best self. The soldier in the movie likens his promise to be faithful to his girlfriend to gold. Yet, "his gold is like yours," Lindo says scornfully to her daughter: "It is only fourteen carats." Lindo is emphasizing that the soldier's promise, like her daughter's, will not be honored. Only twenty-four-carat gold, like a sacred promise, is pure.

By the end of this chapter, the purity of the twenty-four-carat gold parallels the fleshand-blood imagery of the previous section. As An-mei and her mother had to reach deeply into themselves to find their identities, Lindo likewise has had to look deeply within her soul to find her true worth. She realized that the loveless marriage would not destroy her because only she could access her true identity. The twenty-four-carat bracelets symbolize Lindo's true worth, genuine and inviolate. "I remember the day I finally had a genuine thought and could follow it where it went," she says at the end of the chapter. "That was the day I was a young girl with my face under a red marriage scarf. I promised not to forget myself."

Another key theme in this section is that of appearance versus reality. Outside, the Huangs' home appears to be impressive and spacious; inside, it is cramped and uncomfortable. In the same way, Lindo's marriage to the Huangs' son appears to be a step up in the world for her; in reality, she soon realizes that she is doomed to a life of servitude— until she realizes her true, golden worth.

- **the village matchmaker came to my family when I was just two years old . . .**   Many generations ago, most marriages were arranged without the consent of the man and woman involved. The rise of a strong middle class, however, and the growth of democracy gradually brought tolerance for romantic marriages, based on free choice of the partners involved. Nonetheless, arranged marriages are still common in some cultures today, including some Indian cultures and aristocratic families. The most extreme application of the custom of arranged marriages was in pre-revolutionary China; then, a bride and groom often met for the first time on their wedding day.

- **The candle was a marriage bond that . . . meant I couldn't divorce and I couldn't ever remarry, even if Tyan-yu died.**   The traditional Asian value placed on marriage is illustrated in the customs surrounding its dissolution. When one partner dies, for example, widowers and widows must often wait a prescribed time before remarrying; they must also wear mourning clothing and perform ceremonial duties for the dead. While many cultures permit divorce, in some societies divorce is uncommon because it requires the repayment of dowries or other monetary or material exchanges in order to prevent the violation of religious laws. In prerevolutionary China, women were never allowed to remarry, even if their husbands died.

• **When I turned sixteen on the lunar new year . . .** Traditionally, Chinese people reckon their birthdays on the new year. Everyone becomes a year older on the day of the New Year—not on the day they were born. For Chinese people, the year, rather than the month in which a person is born, is important because the Chinese zodiac cycle changes each year.

Ying-ying St. Clair: *The Moon Lady*

The drama in which the Moon Lady is a major character concerns the loss and reclamation of cultural and individual identities. Four-year-old Ying-ying, who has fallen overboard, is desperate to be "found"—to once again be reunited with her family—and with herself. She feels as though she has not only lost her family, but that she has also lost her "self." As an old lady many years later, Ying-ying poignantly tells how she "lost herself." She says that she surrendered her identity as she felt herself being transformed into a shadow, insubstantial and fleeting.

In contrast to that loss and eventual reclamation, Ying-ying explains that today, as an old lady, she realizes that she and her daughter have suffered similar losses, and she wonders if these losses will ever be recovered. She and her daughter can no longer hear one another because Ying-ying rarely voices her thoughts. It was not always so; on the night when she was four years old, she shared her thoughts with the Moon Lady.

The Moon Festival fell on a very hot autumn day. Ying-ying was restless; her nurse (her amah) had dressed her in the heavy silk jacket and pants that Ying-ying's mother had made for her daughter to wear to the Moon Festival. Ying-ying remembers that her amah told her that soon they would see Chang-o, the Moon Lady, who becomes visible on this day only, and when people see her, they can ask for one secret wish to be fulfilled. The Moon Lady is not an ordinary person, the amah explained.

Ying-ying recalls that the departure was delayed because the adults talked. She became increasingly restless until, finally, the servants began to load a rickshaw with provisions, and the family climbed aboard and departed for the river.

Arriving at the lake, they discover that the air is no cooler there than it was inland. The children race around the deck of the floating pavilion, delighting in the ornate decorations, the pretty garden area, and the bustling kitchen. The excitement wanes, however, and after the meal, everyone settles down for a nap. Ying-ying watches some boys send a shackled bird into the water to catch fish. Later, she watches a servant gut fish, chickens, and a turtle, and, with alarm, she realizes that her new outfit is flecked with blood and fish scales. Panicking, she rubs more turtle blood over her clothing, thinking that no one will notice her transformation.

The amah shrieks in terror when she sees Ying-ying covered with blood, but gratefully strips off the soiled garments when she realizes that the child is unharmed.

Alone on the back of the boat in her undergarments, Ying-ying waits as the moon rises. She turns to find the Moon Lady and slips into the water. She is caught in a fishing net and dumped on the deck of another boat. By now, there are so many boats on the water that Ying-ying cannot see her family's boat. She is put on shore, where she watches the Moon Lady performing. Instantly, she is enchanted by the pageant and by the beautiful, soft-spoken Moon Lady. When the play ends, the Moon Lady announces that she will grant a wish. Ying-ying rushes backstage and there, she sees the Moon Lady pull off her hair, drop her gown, and she realizes that the Moon Lady is a man.

Although Ying-ying is rescued by her family, she never believes that she is the same girl. She also forgets many of the details of the day. Today, many years later, when her life is coming to an end, she finally remembers what she asked the Moon Lady: she asked to be "found."

In addition to dealing with the theme of loss, Tan also deals with the concept of the doppelganger. Note that Ying-ying felt that she had surrendered herself "to a shadow, insubstantial and fleeting." Recall, too, the scream of an exploding firecracker and Ying-ying's falling overboard. Stripped of her special tiger clothes and wearing only anonymous cotton undergarments, Ying-ying could be anyone. Indeed, for a moment, she thinks that she may be a little girl on another boat whom she saw, pushing her way through her mother's legs. Ying-ying cried out, "That's not me! . . . I'm here. I didn't fall in the water." The people on the boat laugh at Ying-ying's attempt to understand what has happened.

The phenomenon of the doppelganger, according to psychologists, is fairly common. People feel as though they have met—or seen—their "double," a life-sized mirror image of themselves. Most often, these experiences happen late at night or at dawn and occur during periods of stress and fatigue. This idea of a phantom "double" has existed for centuries. In this case, Ying-ying sees a little girl who is safe; at the same time, she is trying to reinstate herself on shore, as a safe little girl who did *not* fall in the water. She feels that she should be the little girl's "double"—united with her family again, on dry land.

Writers have long used this literary device to probe conflicts within characters, struggles that the characters may not even know they are having. In Dostoevski's *The Double*, for example, a poor clerk sees his double, a man who has succeeded—in contrast to the clerk who has failed. Conrad's *The Secret Sharer* is also built around the notion of a doppelganger. One dark night, a young sea captain rescues a murderer—his double—from the ocean. The captain hides his double and has visions of his own darker side. The narrator of Poe's "William Wilson" is hounded by his double, a man who speaks only in a whisper. Here, Ying-ying is torn between her antithetical desires for both independence and belonging. Like the Moon Lady, she feels as though she doesn't belong anywhere: "In one small moment, we had both lost the world, and there was no way to get it back."

A number of symbols in this section serve to reinforce Tan's themes. First, there is the shadow. "A girl should stand still," Ying-ying's mother admonishes her: "If you are still for a long time, a dragonfly will no longer see you. Then it will come to you and hide in the comfort of your shadow." Later, Ying-ying discovers her shadow, "the dark side of me that had my same restless nature." The shadow here is symbolic of Ying-ying's being pulled between obedience, which leads to her being part of a group, and independence, which leads to isolation. The image of a shadow also echoes the phenomenon of the doppelganger.

In some ways, Ying-ying is like the bird with the ring around its neck, but she is shackled by psychological rather than by physical means. Ying-ying has repressed her identity for so many years that she is unable to communicate with her daughter. This shackle of communication, ironically, yokes the two women, despite the fact that the daughter blocks out her mother's voice by using a mechanical device. She physically closes her ears to Ying-ying's voice with her Sony Walkman and cordless phone. "We are lost, she and I," Ying-ying realizes, "unseen and not seeing, unheard and not hearing, unknown by others." Like the bird, Ying-ying's throat is constricted.

Part II: The Twenty-Six Malignant Gates

A mother cautions her seven-year-old daughter not to ride her bicycle around the corner. When the daughter protests, her mother explains that the child will fall, will cry out—and will be out of earshot. It is all written in a book called *The Twenty-Six Malignant Gates*, the mother explains. The daughter demands to see the book, but her mother says that it would be useless: it is written in Chinese. The daughter then demands to know the twenty-six bad things that can happen, but the mother refuses to answer. In a fury, the girl rushes outside, jumps on her bicycle, and falls—even before she reaches the corner.

This introduction to Part II of the novel reinforces the theme of communication—especially the lack of communication. Mother and daughter are unable to communicate with each other because of barriers in language, personality, and age. The encounter also suggests the theme of control—the mother exerts a seemingly arbitrary power over her daughter. Neither the reader nor the daughter ever finds out why the mother will not allow her daughter to ride her bicycle around the corner. Is the daughter prone to fall? Is there some danger lurking around the corner? When pressed to provide a reason for her refusal, the mother resorts to the unprovable: a book that her daughter cannot read. Perhaps the book symbolizes the unwritten knowledge that all mothers wish to pass on to their daughters; here, the bicycle ride symbolizes the escape that all daughters must make from their mothers.

The last paragraph of this italicized introduction alludes to one of the major themes of the novel. In denying her mother's wisdom ("You don't know anything," the daughter shrieks), the young girl allows us to see the tension between mothers and daughters, between the past and the present, between the Old World and the New World. Each of the daughters in this book learns that her mother does indeed possess great wisdom, learned through great hardship. One of the questions that the book poses is: how can mothers communicate what they know to their daughters? How can they save their daughters the pain that they have experienced?

Waverly Jong: *Rules of the Game*

Waverly Jong, the narrator of this section, explains that she was six years old when her mother taught her "the art of invisible strength," a strategy for winning arguments and gaining respect from others in games. Waverly and her two brothers live on Waverly Place in San Francisco's Chinatown. The children delight in the sights, sounds, and smells of Chinatown, the sweetness of the pasty red beans, the pungent smell of the herbs doled out by old Li, and the sight of the blood-slippery fish that the butcher guts with one deft slice.

Waverly's brother Vincent received a chess set at the Baptist Church Christmas Party. Waverly took to the game immediately, delighting in its strategy. After her brothers lose interest in the game, Waverly learns complex plays from Lau Po, an old man in the park. She begins to win local tournaments. By her ninth birthday, Waverly is a national chess champion. Her fame spreads; even *Life* magazine runs an article on her meteoric rise. Waverly is excused from her chores, but there is one task she cannot escape: accompanying her mother to market on Saturdays. Mrs. Jong delights in walking down the busy street, boasting that Waverly is her daughter. One day, mortified by what she perceives as exploitation, Waverly argues with her mother and dashes off. For two hours, she huddles on an upturned plastic pail in an alley. Finally, she slowly walks home.

Taking their lead from Mrs. Jong, the entire family ignores Waverly, so she trudges to her darkened room and lies down on her bed. In her mind, she sees a chess board. Her opponent consists of two angry black slits, marching implacably across the chessboard and sending her white pieces fleeing for cover. As the black pieces get closer, Waverly feels herself getting lighter. She rises above the board and floats over houses. Pushed by the wind, she ascends into the night sky, alone. Waverly closes her eyes and thinks about her next move.

Tan's first short story was "Endgame." It describes a precocious young chess champion who has a stormy relationship with her over-protective Chinese mother. In 1985, Tan used the story to gain admission to the Squaw Valley Community of Writers, a fiction writer's workshop run by the novelist Oakley Hall. Guided by another novelist and short story writer, Molly Giles, Tan rewrote "Endgame" at the workshop. It was then published in *FM* magazine and reprinted in *Seventeen* magazine. Giles sent the story to Sandra Dijkstra, a literary agent in San Francisco, who thought that it was very well written. When Tan learned that an Italian magazine had reprinted "Endgame" without her permission, she asked Dijkstra to be her agent. Dijkstra agreed. She urged Tan to submit other short stories and to turn the series into a book. That book became *The Joy Luck Club*.

On the surface, "Rules of the Game" applies to the rules of chess, which Waverly masters with astonishing skill. Her success is even more admirable when we realize that she is only eight years old and almost entirely self-taught. Aside from some sessions with old Lau Po in the park, Waverly has taught herself everything that she needs to know about chess in order to become a national champion. She understands the rules of chess. She knows how the game is played and she knows how to psych-out her opponents.

Look, however, at the title from another perspective. In addition to the game of chess, the title alludes to the "game" of life—knowing the "rules" in order to get what you want. Mrs. Jong calls these rules "the art of invisible strength." Unlike the clear-cut rules of chess, however, the rules of the game of life are ever-changing and brutally difficult to learn.

Waverly and her mother struggle for control. Waverly thinks of her mother as an adversary: "I could see the yellow lights shining from our flat like two tiger's eyes in the night,"she says. To Waverly, her mother is like a tiger, waiting to pounce. Predatory, the older woman can destroy with one swipe of her powerful claws. Waverly clearly imagines herself the victim in their struggle. When she reenters the apartment, she sees the "remains of a large fish, its fleshy head still connected to bones swimming upstream in vain escape." Waverly sees herself as the fish, stripped clean by her mother's power, unable to break free.

Waverly, however, is young; she has not realized that as her mother teaches her the "art of invisible strength," Mrs. Jong is equipping Waverly with the very tools she needs to win the battles of life that she will encounter when she grows up. The "art of invisible strength" is self-control. Waverly likens it to the wind, invisible yet powerful beyond belief. The wind can whip up fierce storms and flatten entire communities, yet leave no trace of its presence. In its power and invisibility, it is the strongest of opponents. The "strongest wind cannot be seen," Waverly's chess opponent tells her. Like the human will, it cannot be seen or traced.

In another sense, the "art of invisible strength" represents female power. Women who have been denied conventional paths to power traditionally use their ability to persuade, to shape, and even to control events. If a woman cannot sit in the boardroom, she can shape events from her home—even though a man holds the reins of power. This force is even recognized (and sometimes derided) in the cliché "The woman behind the man."

The "art of invisible strength" is also the power of foreigners, those considered ignorant because they cannot communicate fluently and effectively in the dominant language. For example, Mrs. Jong's fractured English is amusing. When Waverly fears that she will lose a chess match and shame the family, Mrs. Jong says, "Is shame you fall down nobody push you." Under the humor of her syntax, however, her words are powerful and biting—that is, Waverly has no one to blame for her failure but herself. There is nothing humorous in her final comment to Waverly: "We are not concerning this girl. This girl not have concerning for us." With these blunt words, she demonstrates her mastery of the "art of invisible strength." It seems that Mrs. Jong has won this round—or has she?

The struggle for control between Waverly and her mother is symbolized in the dreamlike chess game in the final page of the section. Waverly's opponent in this game is "two angry black slits." When Waverly confronts her mother during their shopping expedition, Mrs. Jong's eyes turn into "dangerous black slits." In the final line of the section, Waverly thinks, "I closed my eyes and pondered my next move." Her mother has taught her to use her *will* to shape events. She now knows that getting what she wants should not be left to fate; rather, she herself can shape events to serve her purpose.

The theme of heritage is also an important element in this section. Mrs. Jong takes great pride in being Chinese. She explains that "Chinese people do many things. Chinese people do business, do medicine, do painting. Not lazy like American people. We do torture. Best torture." Her joy in Waverly's accomplishments is evidence of her great pride. Mrs. Jong delights in showing off her daughter to everyone; Waverly is her legacy to the world. Mrs. Jong feels responsible for her daughter's success. Waverly, on the other hand, thinks that she has accomplished everything on her own. She does not yet understand her mother's point of view.

- **sanddabs**   any of a number of West Coast flatfish.

- *Life* **magazine**   a large format, pictorial newsmagazine. Founded in 1936, it was widely circulated and imitated through the years. Long celebrated for its outstanding photographs and ability to capture the news as it unfolded, *Life* ceased publishing on a weekly basis in 1972.

Lena St. Clair: *The Voice from the Wall*

When she was a child, Lena St. Clair often wondered about a beggar whom her grandfather had sentenced to die in the worst possible way. She imagines all sorts of gruesome torture. Appalled by her interest in violence, her mother said that the way he died didn't matter. Lena thinks that it matters very much because knowing the worst that can happen to you can help you avoid it. The worst thing that happens to Lena is her mother's descent into madness.

Lena traces her mother's madness to a basement in their house in Oakland, California. As a child, Lena broke through a barricaded door and fell headlong into the cellar. To prevent Lena from going into the basement again, her mother told her that a bad man lived down there. After this incident, Lena began to see fantastic, horrible things everywhere.

Lena's mother came to America after World War II as a war bride. At the immigration center, Lena's father renamed his wife "Betty" St. Clair, and two years were subtracted from her age. She looks fearful in the photo of her taken that day, an emotion that remained with her. She cautions Lena about strangers and sees danger in even the most harmless events. Lena's father refuses to learn to speak Chinese, and Mrs. St. Clair cannot learn English. As a result, they have a great deal of trouble communicating. Lena's father puts words into his wife's mouth, but Lena finds out what her mother is really thinking about when they are alone together.

Lena is ten years old when her father is promoted. To mark his success, he moves the family across the bay to San Francisco, where they take an apartment at the top of a steep hill. Mrs. St. Clair is not happy with the apartment, and an encounter with a drunken man upsets her even more. She feels that this apartment is "not balanced" and that all their good luck will vanish. She discovers that she is pregnant, but even this news cannot lift her mood. Meanwhile, Lena listens through the wall to an Italian mother and daughter, Mrs. Sorci and Teresa, arguing and fighting in the adjacent apartment. Their arguments sound so violent that Lena believes that the mother has probably killed her daughter. When she glimpses the daughter a few days later, however, she can't believe that the girl looks so unscathed.

Soon afterward, Mrs. St. Clair loses the baby that she is carrying. In her grief, she cries out about another son whom she thinks that she apparently killed. She then begins to lose her already-fragile grip on reality.

One night, the girl next door knocks on the door of Lena's apartment. Her mother, she says, has kicked her out. She uses the St.Clairs' fire escape to sneak back into her bedroom, and later that night, Lena hears the Italian girl and her mother screaming at each other again. She is astonished when she hears them reconcile and fall into each other's arms with love. Lena dreams of saving her mother from madness.

The theme of heritage is especially important in this section, as Lena explores the dual nature of her identity. The product of an English-Irish father and a Chinese mother, she is a combination of two cultures. Although her pale coloring makes her seem Caucasian, her eyes are unmistakably Chinese. Her nature, like her appearance, straddles two cultures. "I saw these things with my Chinese eyes, the part of me I got from my mother," she says. Like the beggar's death, there are two versions of reality here—Chinese and American. Imaginative, even horrifying visions haunt her; however, her dual vision enables her to maintain her own sanity while watching her mother slide into madness.

When Gu Ying-ying came to America, she was declared a Displaced Person because the immigration officials could not categorize her. Her name was changed to Betty St. Clair, and her birth was postdated by two years. This misclassification is a symbol for her new status: stripped of her Chinese identity, she is, literally, a displaced person, adrift in an alien land. With the erasure of her identity, she has no place in the world. She cannot even communicate with her husband, a well-meaning but insensitive man who refuses to learn Chinese and insists that his wife learn English. When she is unable to communicate, he puts words into her mouth. In effect, he denies her the ability to communicate, and eventually, she descends into madness as a way of dealing with her isolation and loneliness.

The new apartment is a case in point. In an ironic comment, St. Clair announces that his family is "moving up in the world." He imagines this move to be "a move up" in a figurative and literal sense. His new job commands a greater salary, thus enabling him to afford a better home for his family. The family moves up the socioeconomic ladder, and the new apartment is literally perched on the top of a steep hill. The family lives higher up than they were before, but Mrs. St. Clair dislikes the apartment from the start. It is positioned badly, against Chinese nature. "This house was built too steep," she says, "and a bad wind from the top blows all your strength back down the hill." The wind imagery, central to the previous section, recurs here. In "Rules of the Game," the wind symbolized something that could be harnessed to fuel great power. Here, it represents a loss of power. Mrs. St. Clair cannot marshall "invisible strength"; it was taken from her along with her identity. In a vain attempt to realign the family's luck, she rearranges the furniture. Her attempt is a failure, and soon afterward, she loses the baby.

Note Mrs. St. Clair's obsession with rape, birth, and death. In the beginning of the section, she cautions Lena that the bad man in the basement will "plant five babies in her" and then devour her. Later, as she and Lena walk down the street, she cautions Lena to avoid strangers, who will snatch her and "make [her] have a baby." "And then," she adds, "when they find this baby in a garbage can, then what can be done?" The drunken Chinese man who nearly assaults Mrs. St. Clair whispers salaciously of sex. When she loses her baby son, she moans, "I had given no thought to killing my other son!" This utterance tells us that there is a great deal more behind her madness. Something happened in China—something that she cannot express, something which lies hidden behind her agony.

The squabbling between Mrs. Sorci and Teresa is an ironic counterpoint to Lena and her mother's miseries. Lena envies them their battles, their ability to voice their feelings, their love. She wishes that her mother would rant and scream—anything but retreat into the invisible wall of madness. She cries with joy when she realizes the strength of the bond that clasps the feuding Mrs. Sorci and her daughter.

At the end of this section, Lena dreams of a sacrifice that will bring her mother back to sanity. Her dream echoes An-mei Hsu's explanation of her mother's blood sacrifice in "Scar." To save Popo, the daughter slices a section of her arm into the broth. "Even when I was young,"the narrator says, "I could see the pain of the flesh and the worth of the pain." Here, the sacrifice is futile. Horribly painful, it yields no blood nor any shredded flesh. Lena can only dream of its ability to pull her mother through the wall of madness.

Rose Hsu Jordan: *Half and Half*

Rose's mother used to carry a Bible. When she lost her faith, she used the Bible to steady the short leg of the kitchen table. The Bible has remained under the table leg for twenty years.

Tonight, Rose has come to tell her mother that she and her husband, Ted, are getting a divorce. She dreads telling her mother. Rose met Ted Jordan seventeen years ago at the University of California at Berkeley. Initially, she was drawn to his brash, self-assured nature; he was very different from the Chinese boys whom she dated. Rose's mother, Mrs. Hsu, was displeased about the budding relationship because Ted was not Chinese, and Ted's mother, Mrs. Jordan, was displeased because Rose was not American—she was Chinese. At a family picnic, Mrs. Jordan took Rose aside and confided that Ted's future did *not* include a wife who was a member of a minority race.

Hurt and infuriated by Mrs. Jordan's racism, Rose broke up with Ted that evening. Later, they reconciled and were married a month before Ted started medical school. After his graduation, they bought a home, and Rose set up a freelance graphic arts business. Ted made all the decisions in their lives—from what to eat to where to vacation. The marriage was steady until Ted lost a malpractice suit; afterward, he began to press Rose to make some of her own decisions. The marital break came while he was attending a medical convention in Los Angeles. He called late at night and demanded a divorce. Rose lost all faith in Ted's love for her.

She recalls when her own mother lost her faith. One day many years ago, the entire family—parents and seven children—had gone for a day at the beach. Rose was assigned the care of her four brothers—Matthew, Mark, Luke, and Bing. The three elder boys could amuse themselves, but Bing was only four years old and difficult to amuse. Momentarily distracted, Rose's eyes left Bing and he fell into the ocean and drowned.

Everyone took the blame for the tragedy. The next day, Mrs. Hsu returned to the beach with Rose to find Bing. With her Bible in hand, she implored God to return Bing. She even threw her own mother's blue sapphire ring into the ocean as a sacrifice. Finally, with utter despair and horror, she seemed to accept Bing's death.

Rose knows now that her mother never really expected to find Bing—just as she herself knows that she can never save her marriage—even though her mother tells her that she must *try*. She looks into the Bible and discovers that her mother has entered Bing's name under "Deaths"—inscribing it gently, in erasable pencil.

By now you should realize that Tan uses the titles of these various stories to link themes and convey meaning. The title of this particular story, "Half and Half," can be understood on a number of levels, as can the titles that we have encountered so far. As a couple, Ted and Rose are "half and half"—part American, part Chinese. In some instances, a dual heritage can be a source of strength, but not in this particular instance. Together, Rose and Ted do not "fit" into either culture. They are shunned by his mother, who mistakes Rose for Vietnamese—instead of Chinese. Later, she cries bitterly at the wedding, convinced that her son is marrying beneath his social status.

Unlike Mrs. Jordan, Mrs. Hsu is no racist—she is just wary of the foreigner. Cut off from their heritages, Rose and Ted do not unite to create something new, something upon which to build. *The Joy Luck Club* explores the importance of understanding one's heritage as a way of affirming identity. Without her heritage, Rose is like a ghost. Lacking substance, she can but twist in the wind of her husband's decisions and demands.

When Ted abruptly withdraws his support, she is left without balance. "You can't have it both ways, none of the responsibility, none of the blame," Ted screams at Rose. Like Mrs. St. Clair in the previous section, Rose is thrown "off balance." She has nothing to trust—not her husband, not her mother, not even God. There is nothing to prevent her from losing her balance again. "Even if I had expected it, even if I had known what I was going to do with my life," she says, "it still would have knocked the wind out of me." Rose is like the wind; she has no substance.

In contrast, Mrs. Hsu is firmly grounded. Initially, she was supported by her faith. She attended the First Chinese Baptist church every Sunday—until Bing died and she lost her faith. After Bing's death, her Bible becomes a physical, rather than spiritual, prop—a wedge to shore up a rickety table. Ironically, the Bible is still fulfilling its original purpose—"correcting the imbalances of life." On the surface, it seems that Mrs. Hsu is just being practical; after all, why waste a perfectly good Bible? But even twenty years later, the cover is still "clean white,"showing that she hasn't wholly discounted the power of religion to buttress her life. This condition is affirmed when Rose opens the Bible and sees that her mother has entered Bing's name in "erasable pencil." This entry is proof that when she made the entry, she didn't believe that Bing was really dead. She was still hoping that he might return through the power of faith. Even now, she has not reentered his name in ink.

The story of Bing's death parallels Rose's condition. The Hsu family, like Rose and Ted early in their marriage, believed that luck and fate were on their side. Mrs. Hsu strongly believed that she could prevent the tragedies detailed in "The Twenty-Six Malignant Gates" by simply being constantly aware of all of them. Ted believed that he could guide the course of their marriage by making all the right decisions. But Rose and Ted both realized, at last, that life was not as simple as that. There was fate to consider.

Mrs. Hsu mispronounces "faith" as "fate." She attributes their good luck to "faith," only she pronounces it "fate." Rose comes to believe that it was fate—not faith—all along. Their good luck was nothing more than an illusion. Evil is arbitrary and unpreventable. The imagery of the scene of Bing's death reinforces the power of fate's arbitrary hand.

The beach is described as being "like a giant bowl, cracked in half, the other half washed out to sea." This is what will happen to the Hsu family after Bing's death. Moments before the accident, he was sitting "just where the shadows ended and the sunny part began." Like Rose and Ted, he was caught between "half and half," the title of the story.

At the end of the story, Rose concludes that fate "is shaped half by expectation, half by inattention." What remains after tragedy? Faith. This is Mrs. Hsu's reaction to loss, and it is the path that she advises Rose to take. It remains to be seen if Rose can harness the "invisible strength" of the wind that powers Waverly Jong and her mother—or if the wind will sweep her off her feet, off balance.

Jing-mei Woo: *Two Kinds*

To Jing-mei's mother, America is the Land of Opportunity. She has high hopes that her daughter will be a great success as a prodigy. She's not precisely sure where her daughter's talents lie, but she *is* sure that her daughter possesses great ability—it is simply a matter of finding the right avenue for Jing-mei's talents. First, Mrs. Woo tries to mold her daughter into a child actress, but that doesn't work. Then she tries intellectual tests clipped from popular magazines. Jing-mei doesn't show promise in this area, either. Finally, Mrs. Woo hits upon the answer: Jing-mei will be a piano virtuoso.

Mrs. Woo trades housecleaning services for Jing-mei's piano lessons from Mr. Chong, an elderly piano teacher, who is deaf and whose eyes are too weak to tell when Jing-mei is playing the wrong notes. Mr. Chong's efforts are so sincere that Jing-mei picks up the basics, but she is so determined not to cooperate that she plays very badly.

One day, the Woos meet Lindo Jong and her daughter Waverly. Mrs. Jong brags about Waverly's success as a chess prodigy. Not to be outdone, Jing-mei's mother brags about her daughter's "natural pride," and the young girl immediately becomes even more determined than ever to thwart her mother's ambitions.

Continuing to clean houses, Mrs. Woo scrapes together enough money to buy a secondhand piano. A few weeks later, Jing-mei participates in a talent show in a church hall. All the couples from the Joy Luck Club come to her piano debut. Although she has not practiced and does not know the music, Jing-mei has come to believe that she is indeed a prodigy. Halfway through the song, though, she begins to realize how badly she is playing. The weak applause and her parents' disappointed looks reveal the unmistakable truth: Jing-mei is not a musical prodigy.

As a result, Jing-mei is shocked when her mother expects her to continue practicing. During the ensuing quarrel, Jing-mei shouts the most hateful thing she can summon: "I wish I'd never been born! I wish I were dead! Like them!" At the mention of the twin daughters in China that she was forced to abandon years ago, Mrs. Woo suddenly retreats and never mentions the piano again. As a result, Jing-mei is shocked when her mother offers her the piano as a thirtieth birthday present. Only after her mother's death can Jing-mei accept the piano. As she is packing her mother's things, she sits down to play the piano for the first time in many years.

The story focuses on two themes: the American Dream and the tension between mothers and daughters. Like many immigrants, Mrs. Woo believes in America's promise: with hard work and a little luck, Jing-mei can be anything that she chooses to be. Jing-mei will not have to undergo any of her mother's hardships—the terror and privations of war, the tragedy of losing children, and the difficulties of settling in a new culture. It is not enough that Jing-mei be merely successful, however. With her mother's guidance, Jing-mei can be a prodigy, towering above ordinary children. Prodigies, however, are born with an innate talent that manifests itself under the proper guidance, as has Waverly Jong's chess genius. To discover the fallacy of Mrs. Woo's reasoning, all we have to do is contrast Waverly's instant fascination with chess to Jing-mei's refusal to practice the piano. Furthermore, Waverly receives only a few chess pointers from an old man in the park before she begins winning tournaments; in contrast, Jing-mei is given extensive (if inept) personal tutoring, yet she still plays badly in the talent contest.

In addition, Jing-mei has no desire to cooperate with her mother. On the contrary, she fights her every step of the way. "I didn't have to do what my mother said anymore. I wasn't her slave. This wasn't China. I had listened to her before and look what happened. She was the stupid one," she decides. Determined to thwart her mother's ambitions, Jing-mei neglects practicing the piano.

It is only after her mother's death that Jing-mei begins to realize what her mother had wanted for her. She looks back over the music that she formerly shunned and discovers something that she hadn't noticed before. The song on the left-hand side of the page is called "Pleading Child"; the one on the right, "Perfectly Contented." Suddenly, Jing-mei realizes that the two titles are two halves of the same song. This realization brings together the theme of the tension between mothers and daughters. The mothers and daughters in this book are separated by many factors—age, experience, ambition, and culture. The "pleading child" cannot be "perfectly contented" because she cannot resolve her difficulties with her mother—and herself. In her struggle with her mother, she is struggling with her own identity. Who is Jing-mei? Chinese? American? Some combination of the two? She feels that she must reject her mother in order to find herself. Yet in doing so, she is rejecting her heritage and her identity. This book explores the various ways that mothers and daughters relate to each other as the daughters are struggling to forge their own place in the world.

As such, the theme of this story easily transcends the immigrant experience. Children from many cultures and backgrounds steadfastly refuse to believe in their parents' dreams for their future. Whether their parents are on-track or misguided, many children cannot see the value of applying themselves to a goal, practicing a skill, and cooperating with others' plans. In her refusal to accede to her mother's wishes, Jing-mei becomes cruel. She strikes back at her mother with the strongest weapon she can muster—verbally reminding her mother of the central tragedy of her life. And Jing-mei wins the argument—or does she?

Tan also explores the effect of popular culture on the immigrant. Mrs. Woo gets her ideas from television and popular magazines. She does not question the validity of these sources. The magazines range from the bizarre—*Ripley's Believe It or Not*—to the commonplace—*Good Housekeeping* and *Reader's Digest*. Everything has been predigested for mass consumption.

- **Shirley Temple** a famous child actress. Born in 1928, she made her film debut at age three in *Stand Up and Cheer*. Admired for her mop of blond ringlets, her coy, flirtatious pizazz, and her affected, plucky singing and dancing, she became one of the most famous and popular of all child stars in the 30s. Among her best-loved films are *Little Miss Marker* (1934), *The Little Colonel* (1935), *Heidi* (1937), and *Rebecca of Sunnybrook Farm* (1938). She continued to appear in films through her teen years, and after her second marriage, she became active in politics. After an unsuccessful bid for Congress in 1967, she served as a United Nations delegate (1969–70). In 1974, she was named U. S. Ambassador to Ghana. Today, she uses the name Shirley Temple Black.

The Joy Luck Club Genealogy
and Descriptive Map

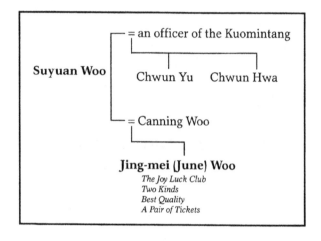

Suyuan Woo

= an officer of the Kuomintang

Chwun Yu   Chwun Hwa

= Canning Woo

Jing-mei (June) Woo
The Joy Luck Club
Two Kinds
Best Quality
A Pair of Tickets

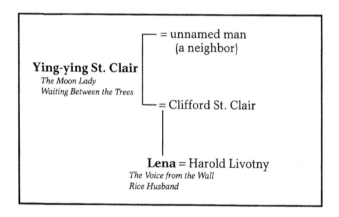

Ying-ying St. Clair
The Moon Lady
Waiting Between the Trees

= unnamed man
(a neighbor)

= Clifford St. Clair

Lena = Harold Livotny
The Voice from the Wall
Rice Husband

= married

Club Genealogy

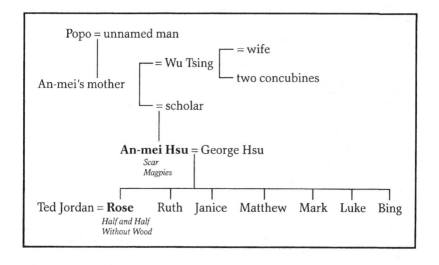

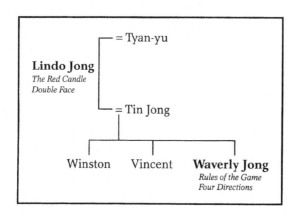

Suyuan Woo started her U.S. Joy Luck Club in 1949, after arriving in San Francisco. "Best Quality" takes place in her home in San Francisco's Chinatown.

An-mei and George Hsu lived in San Francisco's Chinatown before moving south of Golden Gate Park to the Sunset district of San Francisco. South of Sunset is Devil's Slide, where Bing drowns. Their daughter Rose met Ted Jordan at UC Berkeley; Rose first met Ted's mother at a picnic in Golden Gate Park. Ted attended medical school at UC San Francisco. Rose and Ted buy a house in Ashbury Heights, east of Golden Gate Park. Ted calls Rose from Los Angeles and asks for a divorce.

When Ying-ying St. Clair came to the U.S., she was processed through the immigration station at Angel Island and was given the name "Betty." The St. Clairs settled in Oakland's Chinatown; later, they moved across the bay to San Francisco. Their daughter, Lena, marries Harold Livotny and moves to Woodside, a forty-minute drive from her mother's San Francisco apartment.

Lindo and Tin Jong settled in Chinatown; their daughter, Waverly, "Chinatown Chess Champion," was born on Waverly Place. Waverly's first husband, Marvin Chen, attended Stanford on a full scholarship.

Part III: American Translation

A mother is horrified when she discovers that her married daughter has placed a mirrored armoire at the foot of the bed. She is certain that the mirror will deflect all happiness from her daughter's marriage, so she remedies the situation by giving her daughter a mirror to hang above the bed. This arrangement will reverse the bad luck and bring good "peach-blossom luck," the mother says. Such luck, she adds, will ensure a grandchild.

The clash between generations is highlighted in this section. The daughter is upscale and modern. She lives in a condo, not a home. It's an expensive place, boasting a "master suite." She buys elaborate, showy furniture and seems overly concerned with appearance. The mother, in contrast, is steeped in the traditions of the past. She feels that she goes to great lengths to ensure good fortune, for she realizes that fate is capricious and that possessions are not a bulwark against disaster. Unlike her daughter's shallow materialism, the mother wants something of lasting value: grandchildren. Here, again, we encounter the theme of heritage. When the daughter looks in the mirror, she sees herself, suggesting that her children will resemble her, which of course they probably will. This knowledge conveys the link between generations, the ties that bind the past to the present.

- **Price Club** one of a series of enormous warehouse stores. These cavernous stores are stripped of amenities such as dressing rooms, music, fancy displays, and a multitude of salespeople. Sometimes one must belong to a union or other large organization to be a member. There is also a yearly membership fee. Since the stores are so stripped down, their prices tend to be far less than department stores. Like the "twice-used Macy's bag," Tan mentions the store to let the reader know that the mother is very concerned with getting her money's worth. Unlike the daughter, the mother is very thrifty.

Lena St. Clair: *Rice Husband*

Lena believes that her mother has an uncanny ability for predicting bad things that will befall the family. For example, she predicted the failure of a bank and her own husband's death. Lena worries what she will say about the house that Lena and her husband, Harold, have bought in Woodside. What will she predict about their future—based on their new home and the location and arrangement of the rooms in it?

To compound the problem, Lena and Harold are having marital difficulties. At present, the problems are manifesting themselves in a quarrel over who should pay for the cat's flea treatment.

When mother and daughter arrive at the house, Mrs. St. Clair is clearly astonished at the enormous amount of money that her daughter and son-in-law paid for the house. Beneath the fancy architectural details, she sees clearly that the house was vastly overpriced—whereupon, Lena remembers an incident from her childhood.

To coax eight-year-old Lena to finish her food, Mrs. St. Clair told her that her future husband would have one pockmark for every grain of rice that the child did not eat. Little Lena immediately thought of Arnold, a cruel twelve-year-old boy in the neighborhood, who was indeed pockmarked. She quickly finished her rice. The possibility of Arnold being her future husband became a fearful obsession. She hated Arnold so much that she found "a way to make him die." After seeing a movie about lepers in Africa, Lena gradually stopped eating.

One morning when Lena was thirteen, her father read a newspaper article about Arnold's dying of measles. Lena felt that she was somehow responsible for his death. That night, she gorged herself with ice cream. Later, she vomited it up. Her mother discovered her shivering out on the fire escape, hugging the ice cream carton.

Today, Lena knows that she did not cause Arnold's death, but, nonetheless, she feels that she is still being punished. After all, she concludes, she married Harold—not a perfect match.

Initially, Harold Livotny and Lena worked at the same architectural firm, Livotny & Associates. Harold was a partner; Lena, an associate. Lena convinced Harold to start his own firm. He was unwilling to accept money from her to do so, but he did suggest that she move in with him and pay $500 rent—even though the actual rent was $435. She agreed.

The business got off to a rocky start, but with Lena's support and excellent ideas, the firm prospered. Today, Harold makes seven times the amount of money that Lena does, but they still split almost all the expenses down the middle. They have established a detailed, simplistic way to account for their living expenses. Lena's mother is astonished by this detailed accounting. That night, Harold is surprised to learn from Mrs. St. Clair that Lena does *not* like ice cream. Heretofore, he's always made Lena pay fifty-fifty for the ice cream. He's never noticed that Lena never ate any. Is Harold insensitive? You bet.

After her mother goes to bed, Lena initiates an argument with Harold about the way they live. She attempts to redefine their marriage. The argument is interrupted by the sound of glass shattering. The rickety table that Harold designed and made has collapsed and broken a vase in the bedroom where Lena's mother is staying. Upstairs, Lena tells her mother that she knew it would break; her mother asks her: if you knew that this was going to happen, why didn't you do something about what was obviously inevitable?

The table that Harold made as an architectural student is a symbol for Lena and Harold's marriage. Like their relationship, the table is rickety and badly designed—ready to collapse with the slightest provocation. Harold is as oblivious to the table's bad design as he is to the disintegration of his marriage. This fact is evident by the ice cream incident. Harold continues to buy ice cream every week and never notices that Lena never eats any of it. He has no idea that she hates it and that it makes her nauseous. When Mrs. St. Clair points this fact out, Harold completely misinterprets what she is saying. He thinks that she's commenting on Lena's skinny body, that she's made a joke.

Harold is similarly oblivious to the inequality in his relationship with Lena. Under the guise of such modern clichés as "false dependencies," "love without obligation," and "equality," Harold has designed a situation where it's clear to us that Lena has gotten a raw deal. She was co-founder of his architectural firm, providing not only seed money through the rent, as well as constant moral support, but also the creative ideas for the projects. She is the one who thought up the firm's speciality—"theme eating"—which became the underpinning of the business. Yet Harold refuses to recognize her contributions. Indeed, he deliberately prevents her from sharing financial success because he insists on avoiding "favoritism." Lena feels enormous resentment. She likens her husband to Arnold, the pockmarked boy who tormented her as a child. Here, note the similarity between the names "Arn-old" and "Har-old." Finally, Lena regards her husband as another form of punishment that she must endure.

Lena, however, has had problems asserting herself for a long time. As a child, she tried to control her life by restricting the amount of food that she ate. By the time she was a teenager, her obsession with food had turned into anorexia. People who suffer from this condition starve themselves—sometimes to death. It's overwhelmingly a disease of teenage girls. They often eat until they can hold no more food and then make themselves vomit it up. This cycle is called "binging and purging," and that's what Lena did with the ice cream. This behavior often weakens the heart, stomach, and throat. The late singer Karen Carpenter, for example, died of a heart attack in her early thirties from the affects of binging and purging.

Lena is still starving herself. She is so thin, in fact, that her mother complains that she has become "so thin now you cannot see her. She like a ghost, disappear." Harold doesn't notice this, either. Lena tries to blame her inability to assert herself on her background. Being Chinese-American, she thinks, makes her "naturally" timid and prone to having feelings of guilt. Rose, her friend, will have none of this rationalization. Rose says, "Why do you blame your culture, your ethnicity?" Lena suggests that it's a problem that all women of her generation face. "I was reading an article about baby boomers, how we expect the best and when we get it we worry that maybe we should have expected more, because it's all diminishing returns after a certain age," she says. Her mother provides the solution: "Then why don't you stop it?" She is referring, of course, to both the table and the marriage. The table was sure to collapse; the marriage seems doomed to fail. "It's such a simple question," Lena realizes. Yet she backs off from saying what must be said. She initiates the fight with Harold, but collapses into tears before she can fully make her point. Like a ghost, she lacks the strength to save herself.

- **partner/associate** Partners are people who own a percentage of a business. Lawyers, architects, and accountants, for example, are often partners in their business. As partners, they share in a firm's liability. This means that if the firm is sued, for instance, they all are responsible for the costs. Partners take this risk because they usually make much more money than associates. Associates are salaried employees. They get a set amount of money each pay period—no matter how much money the firm makes.

- **baby boomers** people born between 1946 and 1964. Raised during the affluent post-World War II period, many of these people have high expectations for material success. Some of them, however, like Lena, have discovered that material success does not ensure happiness; they find their lives empty and unsatisfying. Others, like Harold, are very satisfied with the fruits of their labors—he is proud of his fine house and his Jaguar automobile. A baby boomer herself, Tan is especially sensitive to this dichotomy.

Waverly Jong: *Four Directions*

Waverly Jong takes her mother out to lunch, planning to break the news that she and Rich Schields are getting married. The lunch goes badly, however, and Waverly does not tell her mother about the upcoming marriage. Waverly is afraid of her mother's disappointment and censure. When Waverly's friend Marlene suggests that Waverly and Rich elope, Waverly explains that she eloped with her first husband, and the marriage was a disaster. Her mother threw her shoe at them—and that was just for starters.

To allow her mother an opportunity to realize that Waverly and Rich are already living together, Waverly invites her mother back to her apartment. It is cluttered with her daughter Shoshana's toys and Rich's clothes and barbells. Waverly opens a closet and shows her mother the mink jacket that Richard gave her for Christmas. Mrs. Jong's comment makes Waverly feel that the gift is shabby; she makes no mention of the fact that Waverly and Rich are obviously living together. Waverly recalls another time when her mother hurt her.

That time, Waverly insulted her mother on Stockton Street and hid in the alley for hours. To retaliate against her mother for bragging about Waverly's outstanding chess playing, Waverly decided to quit the game. Even that ploy, however, didn't thaw the chill between them, so Waverly returned to chess. Mrs. Jong seemed unconcerned, yet she tenderly nursed Waverly through her bout with chicken pox.

Waverly realized then that she had erected a wall between herself and her mother. To her horror, Waverly began to lose tournaments. She lost her feeling of supreme confidence. She was terrified that she would no longer be a prodigy and would become someone ordinary. She quit chess for good when she was fourteen years old.

Now, Waverly is afraid that her mother will point out Rich's flaws and turn him into something ordinary. This is what happened to Waverly's feelings for her first husband, Marvin Chen. Waverly concocts a plan: her mother will cook dinner for her and Rich.

At the end of the evening, Rich is sure that he has "passed the test," but Waverly knows that he failed miserably. The next day, angry at what she perceives as her mother's manipulations, Waverly decides to tell her mother that she and Rich are getting married.

Her mother is kind and understanding, which puzzles Waverly and she bursts into tears. They talk and Waverly finally sees that her mother does indeed love her. She had only been waiting for Waverly to "let her in" to her world. Waverly and Rich postpone their wedding until October, so that they can honeymoon in China in the cooler season. Waverly thinks it would be disastrous—yet wonderful—if her mother would go with them.

Here, we see that this chapter picks up the conflict described in "Rules of the Game"—that is, Waverly's love/hate relationship with her mother. Waverly is now an adult. She is a highly successful tax attorney in a high-powered position. According to her friend Marlene, Waverly is so assertive that she does not even have a problem taking on the IRS. Nonetheless, all of that power dissolves when she has to deal with her mother. She becomes a child again in her mother's presence. Her mother seems all-powerful, and Waverly feels that she must continually prove her worth to her mother. She feels that her mother poisoned her first marriage—and, now, she will not get married again until she gets her mother's approval. She cannot even imagine eloping—even though it is her second marriage. Marlene is astonished that Waverly has difficulty telling her mother that she is getting married. Even Rich is amazed. "How long does it take to say, Mom, Dad, I'm getting married?" he asks jokingly. Because of Waverly's dependence, her mother still has the power to change Waverly's perception of reality.

Waverly adores Rich. He loves her unconditionally and makes her happy in every way. "I had never known love so pure," she says. Yet when she senses that her mother does not approve of Rich, her own opinion of him sours. Rich tumbles from being a sort of god to being an animal. "He had the look of a Dalmatian, panting, loyal, waiting to be petted," she says in disgust.

Tan uses a chess metaphor to explain Waverly's feelings and her battle with her mother. "In her hands, I always became the pawn. I could only run away. And she was the queen, able to move in all directions, relentless in her pursuit, always able to find my weakest spots." In addition to figuratively expressing Waverly's relationship with her mother, this metaphor also serves to unify the structure of the book. It continues the chess metaphor central to "Rules of the Game" and, thus, it links the two stories.

Notice, however, that nowhere has Mrs. Jong directly criticized Rich: the perception of maternal disapproval is all in Waverly's mind. For example, Waverly interprets her mother's remark about Rich's freckles—which she herself elicited—as an insult. Waverly responds to her mother's remark "a bit too heatedly." Clearly she is looking for a confrontation. Similarly, the Jongs do not criticize Rich's clumsy attempt to use chopsticks or his gauche gift of wine— only Waverly does. In the same way, Rich has no way of knowing that Mrs. Jong, by tradition, criticizes her own cooking as a way of eliciting compliments. Waverly is horrified when Rich agrees with Mrs. Jong's criticism about her famous steamed pork and preserved vegetable fish. Yet, because Waverly did not brief Rich about her mother's habits, it almost seems as if Waverly was waiting for him to fail. This behavior is called a "self-fulfilling prophecy." Waverly has decided what her view of the world is, collected information to support it, and finally shared her view with others as "truth." In communicating this way, people can actually change their own behavior, and that of others, so that the result affects their own distorted view. Waverly is so busy finding fault with Rich that she does not even realize that her mother has already acknowledged their love, as well as their probable plans to marry. In a fury, Waverly rushes over to her mother's house to assert herself.

What she sees amazes her. Her mother is not the monster that she imagined. Rather, the old woman seems innocent and childlike. Waverly is pulled apart by her contradictory emotions and perceptions. Recall that the title of this story is "Four Directions." Waverly has difficulty telling appearance from reality because she is pulled in different directions by her own preconceptions, misconceptions, and memories of the past. She is pulled in two directions by her Chinese heritage and American ways. Her mother realizes this dilemma: ". . . if you are Chinese you can never let go of China in your mind," she says. Her mother has been waiting for Waverly to let her in, to accept her Chinese heritage so that she can accept Waverly's Chinese-American future, symbolized by Waverly's daughter, Shoshana. At the end of the chapter, Waverly finally realizes this truth. She imagines what it might be like to travel back to China with her mother, to "move West to reach East."

- **IRS** the popular name for the Internal Revenue Service. Empowered by the U. S. government to collect taxes, the IRS has traditionally triggered fear because of its power to examine tax records, impose fines, and seize property to pay off tax money owed. Tan likens Mrs. Jong to the IRS to humorously illustrate how much Waverly fears her.

- **pawn** one of eight chess figures of one color; it has the lowest power and value. Pawns are usually moved one square at a time vertically; they capture diagonally. The word has come to mean a person who is used or manipulated to further another person's purposes.

- **queen** the most powerful chess piece of either color. The queen can move any unobstructed distance in any direction.

Rose Hsu Jordan: *Without Wood*

As a child, Rose believed everything that her mother told her. A timid youngster, she resisted sleep, fearing nightmares. Her mother told her that Old Mr. Chou guarded the door to dreams. One night, she dreamed that she was in Old Mr. Chou's nighttime garden, where he chased her through the garden, shouting, "See what happens when you don't listen to your mother!"

Thirty years later, Rose's mother is still trying to make her daughter listen. They meet at the funeral for China Mary, a mother who has helped many children in the neighborhood. Rose's mother criticizes Rose for being too thin and for confiding in her psychiatrist rather than in her own mother. Later, Rose considers what her mother said. She realizes that she has been feeling confused, caught in a dark fog of conflicting emotions.

Rose has been telling her friends different versions of her breakup with Ted. For example, Rose told Waverly about the physical pain of divorcing Ted; she told Lena that she feels relieved to be free of him. She told her psychiatrist that she wants revenge—yet, despite her vivid descriptions of revenge, her psychiatrist looks bored.

To settle her conflicting emotions, Rose views all the possessions that she and Ted amassed during their marriage. Soon afterward, Ted sends her a check for $10,000, along with the divorce papers. Is Ted trying to trick her into accepting this money as a full settlement? Is he saying that he still loves her? Unable to decide how to handle the check and papers, Rose stuffs them in a drawer. Her mother once explained Rose's penchant for indecision by saying that Rose was "without wood." Lacking this sturdy fiber, Rose bends in all directions—she cannot stand alone, cannot take a stand for herself.

Rose walks in the garden, a once-immaculate assortment of flowers and herbs, now gone wild from neglect. She then goes to bed and stays there for three days. On the fourth day, she has a nightmare about Old Mr. Chou and awakens when her mother calls her on the telephone. Ted phones and presents his demands. Anxious to remarry, he wants the divorce papers signed immediately, and he also wants the house as part of the settlement. Rose breaks into gales of laughter when she realizes that Ted has been having an affair. She invites him to come over that night, with no idea about what she is going to say.

She ends up showing him the overgrown garden. As they walk through the plants, she hands him the unsigned divorce papers and announces that she will *not* move out of the house. That night, she dreams of her mother and of Old Mr. Chou and his garden. In the garden, she discovers her mother tending a wild sea of weeds that, she boasts, she herself planted.

Vividly, this section describes how Rose finally finds her "voice," her identity, and the ability to trust herself. From early childhood, Mrs. Hsu attempted to teach her daughter to listen to her and, thus, to learn how to listen to herself. But Rose was a timid child, unsure of where to find the truth, and she grew into a timid woman, uncertain of herself and unwilling to make decisions. Eventually, her indecision frustrated her husband, and the couple grew apart. In her mother's words, Rose was "without wood," lacking both strength and substance. She rejected her mother's wisdom and looked to Americans' opinions of her.

This characterization echoes Tan's own rejection of her mother and her heritage. "I felt ashamed of being different and ashamed of feeling that way," Tan said in an interview in the *Los Angeles Times*. By the time that Tan was an adolescent, she rejected everything Chinese. It was only after she matured that she returned to her heritage, much like her fictional creation, Rose. "It was only later that I discovered there was a serious flaw with the American version," Rose says. "There were too many choices."

Tan uses two important symbols to represent Rose's maturation. The first is the flower and herb garden that Ted had been cultivating. A garden is a traditional symbol for growth and rebirth, and as in the Bible, this garden will serve as a backdrop for betrayal. When Rose and Ted were happily married, Rose loved the house and the manicured garden. She thought that it was an outward manifestation of the healthy flowering of her marriage. It was their Garden of Eden, perfect and without sin. In reality, it was little more than another sign of her husband's obsessive nature. Every weekend, he sorted and pruned the plants, much as he controlled Rose's life. He rejected anything that could not be categorized—like the cutting of aloe vera that Lena gave Rose: there was no room for this stray, single succulent in Ted's garden. Everything had its ordained place in Ted's orderly world view. Like a god, he controlled it all. With Ted's departure, the garden went to ruin, much as Rose's life fell into disarray. The calla lilies languished, the daisies drooped— much like Rose, who felt defeated by the sudden loss of Ted's emotional support. Like the flowers, she was unable to hold up her own head and face the world. Her very name—Rose—reinforced her place within Ted's garden. And, as in the Garden of Eden, there was a snake in Ted's garden: Ted himself. As Rose's mother suspected, Ted has been "doing monkey business" for quite some time. Now he wants a divorce so that he can marry his lover. And Rose would probably have given him, dutifully, what he wanted—had she not strolled into the garden and looked closely at it.

Initially appalled by the clumps of weeds, she rushes to the garden shed for pesticides and weed killers. But this urge doesn't feel right; she has the sense that someone is laughing at her. Rose realizes that she doesn't want to get rid of the weeds. Instead, she goes to call the lawyer—to seek outside help. But this notion is not right either. She suddenly breaks down emotionally and takes to her bed. When she is awakened—significantly, by her mother's call to life—Rose realizes that she can survive without Ted. This is where Tan emphasizes another key symbol, the weeds. Rose is no longer the delicate flower that her name suggests. Now she is a weed—a tough survivor. The weeds in the garden have sprouted up in the patio cracks, anchoring themselves in the side of the house and spreading under the loose shingles. Weeds are strong, Rose realizes—so strong, in fact, that they are capable of burying themselves in the very foundation of a house. When that happens, you have no choice but to pull down the building. Like the weeds, Rose has taken root in the foundation of her home. She has no intention of relinquishing it to Ted. It is hers; he will have to tear it down to get it away from her.

The dream sequence at the chapter's close reinforces this symbol of Rose's new-found identity and strength. In the dream, Rose's mother is walking with Old Mr. Chou through the foggy garden. Notice that Rose is no longer afraid of Old Mr. Chou, her longtime enemy. She now welcomes sleep because she is in touch with her inner self. She is at peace. And her mother is planting weeds! This is an inversion of our expectations. People plant flowers; they pluck weeds. But Rose's mother realizes the strength of weeds. They aren't fragile roses that wither in the glaring sun or driving rain; they are hearty survivors. In the garden, they are already "spilling out over the edges and running wild in every direction." Like them, Rose has taken root. Like the tough weeds, she can now survive life's blows.

Jing-mei Woo: *Best Quality*

After a Chinese New Year's dinner, Jing-mei's mother gave her a jade pendant which she said was her "life's importance." At first, Jing-mei did not like the pendant; it seemed too big and ornate. After her mother's death, however, the pendant will begin to assume great importance to her—even though she does not really understand the meaning that her mother assigned to it. Later, Jing-mei will notice other Chinese wearing similar pendants and she will ask one of them what the pendant signifies. He won't know either.

Jing-mei had helped her mother shop for the crabs that she served at the New Year's dinner. That day, her mother was annoyed about the tenants living in the second-floor apartment of a six-unit building that she owns. She was especially bothered by their cat, which Jing-mei and the tenants suspect that she poisoned. Jing-mei listened patiently to her mother as she poked the crabs to find the liveliest ones. As she was spearing the live crabs from the tank, one of them lost a limb. Mrs. Woo refused to accept it because a maimed crab is bad luck for the New Year. After a lengthy discussion, the fishmonger threw it in for free. When they return home, Jing-mei watches her mother cook, but she leaves the room when Mrs. Woo begins to boil the crabs; she cannot bear to see them die.

There are eleven people at the New Year's celebration. Mrs. Woo hadn't counted Waverly's daughter, Shoshana, and so she purchased only ten whole crabs. When she sees the extra person, she decides to cook the eleventh crab, the one missing a limb. At dinner, Waverly takes the best crab for her child, and Mrs. Woo ends up with the maimed one, which she doesn't eat.

Waverly subtly insults Jing-mei during the dinner, mentioning her choice of hairdresser. Jing-mei retaliates by teasing Waverly about her firm's finances because the bill that Jing-mei submitted for her ad copy has not been paid. Waverly retorts that Jing-mei hasn't been paid because her work was not acceptable—a retort that reduces Jing-mei to tears. Auntie Lindo comes to Jing-mei's rescue, pleading with Waverly to let Jing-mei rewrite the material. Waverly ignores her. Jing-mei goes to wash the dishes; she is no longer angry at Waverly—she simply feels tired and foolish.

Later that night, after everyone has left, Jing-mei asks her mother why she did not eat her crab. Her mother tells her that it was already dead before she cooked it and, thus, it was not edible. She cooked it merely because she thought that it *might* still be good and because she knew that only Jing-mei would pick it, because Jing-mei would never choose the "best quality." She sees this virtue as one of Jing-mei's best qualities. Then she gives to Jing-mei her "life's importance," the jade pendant necklace.

Note that the last section of this chapter is set in the present. Jing-mei is cooking dinner for her father, who has not been eating well since his wife's death. She hears the tenants upstairs and now understands her mother's former complaints. The tenant's cat appears at the window, and Jing-mei realizes that her mother did not poison it, after all.

In part, this novel's richness comes from its ability to make the specific general. We see this illustrated best in Jing-mei's experiences. Jing-mei, like many people, is satisfied with less than "best quality." She is so self-effacing that she sacrifices for others without even thinking about her actions. Not being fond of crab, she nonetheless, automatically, reaches for the least desirable crab—the one with the missing leg—during the New Year's dinner. She does not think herself worthy of the best. Clearly, however, this admirable selflessness also has a destructive side. Jing-mei is easily humiliated by those who possess a greater deal of self-confidence—such as her childhood friend Waverly Jong. During Jing-mei's childhood, her mother had tried to make her into a child prodigy like Waverly, the childhood chess champion. All of Mrs. Woo's efforts failed. Waverly became a successful tax accountant for a major firm; Jing-mei, a copywriter for a small advertising firm. Jing-mei is awed by Waverly's great economic success. She sees this material success as proof of Waverly's greater worth as a person.

Jing-mei's mother does not value Waverly so highly. She sees Waverly as a crab, scuttling in a rut. "Why you want to follow behind her, chasing her words?" Mrs. Woo scolds. "She is like this crab . . . always walking sideways, moving crooked. You can make your legs go the other way." Mrs. Woo believes that her daughter has freedom of choice, the ability to think for herself and go against the tide of convention. Jing-mei, she believes, is a leader—not a follower. Mrs. Woo gives her the jade necklace in order to bequeath this belief to her daughter. This necklace, worn against the skin, will hopefully transfer the family heritage from mother to daughter.

Perhaps Jing-mei is correct in believing that her mother gives her the necklace, in part, to soothe her humiliation. Perhaps, however, Mrs. Woo foresees her own death, only months from now. The maimed crab, "a bad sign at Chinese New Year," might herald her end. Perhaps it is a combination of both factors, as well as Mrs. Woo's desire to impress upon her daughter that she is "best quality," worthy of the best that life has to offer. She should no longer be satisfied with the leavings of others; it's time that she herself reach for the best. Mrs. Woo is offering love and confidence to her daughter. These two character assets are her heritage to her.

Tan's subtle humor is evident when Mrs. Woo smugly recounts to Jing-mei how she got the better of one of her tenants. To retaliate, the tenant called her "the worst Fukien landlady." She complacently tells Jing-mei that he was wrong—she is *not* from Fukien. She mistook the obscenity for a Chinese city and thus completely missed the point of his insult. In effect, she won this skirmish—because she misunderstood his insult.

• **jade** a gemstone that ranges in color from dark green to almost white.

In ancient times, it was used for weapons, utensils, and ornaments. Today, it is used for rings, necklaces, earrings, and other articles of jewelry. Jade has always been prized by the Chinese as the most precious of all stones. The finest quality jade carvings come from China.

- **tofu** bean curd. The small white squares have a soft, spongy texture and a bland taste. Tofu is considered a nutritious food because it is an excellent source of protein, is fat free, and low in calories. Tofu can be eaten plain, but it is usually cut into small squares and used in lieu of meat, fish, or chicken in stir-fry recipes. It can also be used in making cold salads. Tofu is often sold in deli departments of large supermarkets or small food specialty stores.

- **AIDS** Waverly says that because Jing-mei's hairdresser is gay, he *could* have AIDS. He is cutting hair, "which is like cutting a living tissue." There has not been a single reported case of anyone contracting AIDS through a haircut; this scene is proof that Waverly can be prejudiced, misinformed, and even cruel.

Part IV: Queen Mother of the Western Skies

As she plays with her granddaughter, an old woman wonders what she will teach the child. The old woman recalls that she too was once free and innocent, laughing for sheer pleasure. Later, she threw away her innocence to protect herself. She taught her daughter to do the same. She wonders now if "this way of thinking" is wrong, for now she sees the evil in the world. She teases the baby, calling her "Syi Wang Mu," Queen Mother of the Western Skies, and she asks for the answer to her question. Continuing the game, she thanks the Little Queen and asks her to teach her daughter how to lose her innocence—but not her hope—for then, this baby's mother will be able to laugh forever.

The interplay here between innocence and experience is a key theme in literature. It lies at the heart of Homer's *Odyssey*, John Milton's *Paradise Lost*, William Blake's "Songs of Innocence and Experience," and Jonathan Swift's *Gulliver's Travels*. In each case, the author examines how characters react to losing their innocence.

In this novel, the mothers—Suyuan Woo, An-mei Hsu, Lindo Jong, and Ying-ying St. Clair—all experienced almost undescribable horrors during their lifetimes. They have learned first-hand that the world can be a terribly dangerous place—and they have paid for this knowledge with the loss of their innocence. Because of this loss, they now see evil everywhere, and they wonder if they have become evil through association. This awareness too often robs them of their laughter.

The grandmother wishes that there were a way to teach women how to be aware of the world's evil—yet allow them to maintain their hope for future happiness. This way, they would not be hurt—and they could laugh forever. This lesson is what each of the women in the Joy Luck Club has tried to teacher her daughter.

• **Buddha** Siddhartha Gautama, a young prince born in 563 B.C., near the present-day India-Nepal border. When he was twenty-nine years old, he embarked on a quest for peace and enlightenment and renounced all earthly pleasures. Eventually, however, he adopted a middle path between self-indulgence and self-denial. Sitting under a bo tree meditating, he rose through levels of consciousness until he reached the state of enlightenment that he had been seeking. He then began to teach. Buddhism, one of the major religions in the world, developed from his teachings. Today, an estimated 150–300 million people are Buddhist. Scholars estimate that the number may be much higher in China, but the country does not recognize any religion.

An-mei Hsu: *Magpies*

To her mother (An-mei), Rose reveals that her marriage is falling apart. Paralyzed with grief and indecision, Rose can do nothing but weep. An-mei understands that by refusing to do something decisive about this problem, Rose is, in effect, choosing to do nothing. She knows that her daughter must make a choice: Rose must try to assert herself or she will lose her chance forever. An-mei understands this character flaw because she herself was taught to demand nothing for herself.

An-mei remembers sixty years ago, when she first saw her mother. An-mei's mother had returned home when her own mother, Popo, lay dying. After Popo died, An-mei's mother prepared to leave. On the eve of her departure, she told An-mei a story from her childhood, when she was a little girl about An-mei's age. Her mother, Popo, told her that she could no longer be a child. From this experience, An-mei's mother learned that it is useless to cry, for tears only feed someone else's joy.

On the morning of her departure, An-mei's mother suddenly

takes An-mei with her. On the long journey, she entertains the little girl with stories about the wonders that the child will encounter. On the morning of their arrival, An-mei's mother shocks her daughter by discarding her white mourning dress for Western-style clothes. She has a fine dress for An-mei, too, and explains that they will live in the home of Wu Tsing, a rich merchant.

Despite her description of the wealth that awaits them, An-mei is stunned by the lavish Western-style house and by the scores of servants that she sees. She learns about First Wife, Second Wife, Third Wife, and about her mother—Fourth Wife. At first, little An-mei is delighted by her new home, but about two weeks later, she begins to understand her mother's lack of status in this new household.

Old Wu Tsing arrives with his fifth wife, a woman only a bit older than nine-year-old An-mei, who suddenly realizes that something is wrong here. A few nights later, An-mei is awakened when Wu Tsing comes to her mother's bed. The child is taken to a servant's bed for the night. That afternoon, for the first time, An-mei's mother tells the child about her deep sorrow. As Fourth Wife, she has almost no status within the household.

Soon afterward, the other wives return. First Wife is a plain, honest woman; Second Wife is full of treachery. She gives An-mei a string of pearls to win her affection. To counter Second Wife's trickery, An-mei's mother crushes one of the pearls beneath her feet. The child sees instantly that the pearls are false. From then on, she learns more and more about the wives and their various powers.

First Wife has the most power by virtue of her position, but her spirit was broken after the birth of her first child, who was born with one leg shorter than the other. Her second child had a large birthmark over half her face. First Wife now spends her time going to Buddhist temples seeking cures for her children. She has her own home—and thus, An-mei's mother also wants *her* own home. Second Wife was a sing-song girl who knows how to control men. To get an increase in her allowance, she feigns suicide by swallowing a piece of raw opium. She continues this ploy until she gets everything she wants—but she cannot have children; therefore, she arranged for Wu Tsing to take a third wife, who gave birth to three daughters. Later, Second Wife arranged for An-mei's mother to become Fourth Wife by tricking her into staying the night, whereupon Wu Tsing raped her. She later gave birth to a son, which Second Wife claimed as her own.

Two days before the New Year, An-mei's mother poisons herself with opium. Empowered by her action, An-mei crushes the pearl necklace that Second Wife gave her. Now, An-mei wants her daughter to stand up for herself and stop suffering in silence.

The story of An-mei's mother is based on truth. Tan's maternal grandmother, Jing-mei, had been widowed after her husband, a scholar, died. A wealthy womanizer forced her into concubinage by raping her. Society and her family cast her aside in horror. In an article that Tan wrote for *Life* magazine in April 1991, she explained that Jing-mei "killed herself by swallowing raw opium buried in the New Year's rice cake." After her mother's death, Daisy (Amy's mother) married her abusive first husband in China and had three daughters. Amy and her two brothers are children from Daisy's second marriage.

This story focuses on power—its use and abuse. Wu Tsing and the system that he represents have abused women for centuries. As a widow, An-mei's mother had no value at all, despite such traditional female assets as beauty and refinement. Notice that she does not even have a name, for she has no identity of her own. But she refuses to be defeated by the system. By killing herself, she effects a change in her daughter, giving her the power to rebel. She makes this stand clear to An-mei: "When the poison broke in her body, she whispered to me that she would rather kill her own weak spirit so she could give me a stronger one." An-mei seized power from her mother's sacrifice. By crushing the false pearls, she is announcing her independence. This action is echoed in the actions of the Chinese peasants at the end of the chapter. For thousands of years, they have been tormented by birds. Finally, they rise up and beat the birds back. "Enough of this suffering and silence!" they shout—and beat the birds to death.

In the same way, Tan suggests, women must rise up and beat back oppressive systems, especially male-dominated ones. An-mei's daughter, Rose, has been defeated by her marriage to Ted, but there is no need for such misery today, her mother says. Rose should stop pouring out her tears to the psychiatrist—just as An-mei should not have cried to the turtle. Such tears only feed someone else's joy. Instead, Rose should assert herself, as An-mei has done. As we know from the section entitled "Without Wood," Rose does indeed stand up to Ted. "You just can't pull me out of your life and throw me away," she says. She refuses to sign the divorce papers and move out of their home.

In a sense, both An-mei and Rose have remade themselves, invented new identities to survive. Tan reinforces this concept of strength by having the trip to Tientsin take seven days, the same number of days as in the Hebrew myth of creation. Notice also how she interweaves the theme of appearance and reality. It appears that An-mei's mother is a "fallen woman," but in reality, she was trapped by rape and a vicious social system. An-mei believed that Second Wife was kindly, but she is full of evil. The child assumed that the pearls were real; they were but glass. Tan inverts the symbol of the magpie to reinforce this theme. "Magpie" is the common name for members of the crow family. The birds are found in North America, Asia, Europe, and northwestern Africa. Chinese people traditionally regard the bird as a symbol of joy. Tan, however, inverts the symbol, using it in the Western sense as a harbinger of evil. The birds destroy crops and must be beaten back. So also must women cry out against evil and fight for what is right for them.

Ying-ying St. Clair: *Waiting Between the Trees*

Lena St. Clair has put her mother in the guest bedroom, the smallest room in the house. Mrs. St. Clair is upset because her daughter does not understand that the guest bedroom should be the *best* one in the house. To Mrs. St. Clair, her daughter's house looks as though it will break into pieces.

Mrs. St. Clair recalls that she was a wild girl in her youth. Her mother said that she would bring shame to their house, but Ying-ying disregarded these warnings. Her family was one of the richest in Wushi, but the wealth meant little to young Ying-ying. She played on the street with a priceless jade jar, treating it like a toy. When she was sixteen, her aunt married. After the festivities, a male friend of the family humiliated Ying-ying by plunging a knife into a watermelon, a crude symbol suggesting the loss of virginity. Six months later, Ying-ying married this man and fully understood his cruel taunt.

The night of her aunt's wedding was also important to Ying-ying because it was then that she first began to know about things before they happened. It was then that she knew that she would marry the crude man who plunged the knife into the watermelon. Ironically, after they were married, Ying-ying began to love him. It happened one afternoon when he said that she had tiger eyes. Soon afterward, she became pregnant—and discovered that her husband had left her for an opera singer. She had an abortion, and in her grief, she went to live with a second cousin's family. They were terribly poor, but she stayed ten years amid the squalor. Then she moved to the city and became a shop girl. There, she met Clifford St. Clair; she knew at once that they would marry. For four years, he courted her, buying her little trinkets, which meant nothing to her when she set them against the riches she had known. But, nonetheless, she saved the baubles because she knew that she would marry St. Clair. One day, she received a letter saying that her husband was dead, and she decided to let St. Clair marry her. On the day that her daughter was born, she brought out the trinkets he had given her. He adored her, but she loved him only as a ghost would love, without feeling. She had lost her *chi*, her spirit.

To regain her spirit, Ying-ying is going to confront her past. This pain will free her spirit so she can cut her daughter's spirit free. Like a tiger, Ying-ying sits and waits for her daughter.

The Joy Luck Club has been lavishly praised for its literary techniques. One of the most successful aspects of Tan's techniques is her use of multiple points of view. Notice how Tan retells each story from the mothers' and daughters' points of view. This interweaving of viewpoints underscores the difficulty that the mothers and daughters have communicating with one another. How *could* they fully understand each other when each is getting only half the story? Shifting viewpoints also serves to unify the book, develop themes, and heighten reality.

This story alludes to Lena St. Clair's "Rice Husband." There, the narrator is Lena. She opens her story with a description of her mother's ability to see things before they happen. This foreshadows Ying-ying's discovery of Lena's misery. Like Ying-ying, Lena has become a ghost. Both women are suffering from a secret sorrow—the same sorrow. They have made miserable marriages. Ying-ying lost her beloved first husband to another woman and was able to love her second husband only after he died. Lena has subordinated her spirit to her husband and bitterly resents his domination.

Ying-ying sees her daughter's misery; Lena's husband Harold does not. Lena is similarly blind to the reality of her mother. She has no idea of her mother's past. She does not suspect that her mother was once married to another man; she has no inkling that her mother had an abortion. She believes that her father rescued her mother from a poor village; she never imagines that her mother was raised in great wealth. She sees only a frail old lady, not a vigorous, clever tiger. Both stories end the same way; with the poorly balanced table, a symbol of their lives, crashing to the floor.

The symbolism of this story reinforces the theme of appearance and reality. Lena appears to be happy, but she is miserable. Ying-ying appears to be a frail old lady, but she is really a tiger. The tiger itself is a symbol of duality. The gold and black creature has two sides. The gold side represents its fierce heart; the black side, its cunning and stealth. Like a tiger, Ying-ying appears to be asleep when she is awake. She "has one eye asleep, the other open and watching." Notice how the clever naming of Ying-ying's second husband also emphasizes duality. The "St." appears to be a martyr, rescuing his poor wife from a wretched life of misery. Yet it was Ying-ying who decided that it was time to marry—not St. Clair.

Even the symbol of the knife and watermelon suggests duality. Ying-ying's first husband plunged the knife into the watermelon to make a crass joke about her virginity. Later, the same symbol represents her abortion.

The other primary theme of this section is that strength lies in confronting the past. That is what Lena has begun to do in "Rice Husband," as she evaluates her life with Harold. She realizes that she has sold herself short, that she deserves far better than she has gotten. Here, Ying-ying determines to gather the threads of her past and use them as tools to cut her spirit loose. When she has once again regained her *chi*, her spirit, she can penetrate her daughter's hide and cut *her* tiger spirit loose. Ying-ying is aware that there will be a struggle, but she is confident that she can win. Freeing her daughter's strength will be her legacy.

Tan uses humor to relieve the seriousness of these themes. For example, Ying-ying calls her son-in-law "Arty-tecky" for "architect." Lena laughs at the mispronunciation; the reader laughs because we know that Lena and Harold are indeed "arty." They are shallow people taken in by trends. They pay far too much money for "hand-bleached floors" and "marbleized walls." Ying-ying's comments about "so-so security" are also humorous. The social security payments *are* really "so-so," for they do not provide enough money for her security.

Lindo Jong: *Double Face*

Waverly wants to go to China for her honeymoon, but is afraid that she will blend in so well that she will not be allowed to return to America. Her mother reassures her that there is no chance that she will be mistaken for a Chinese citizen. Waverly is American. Lindo tried to give her children the best of Chinese and American cultures, but she did not realize that the two ingredients did not mix.

In preparation for her wedding to Rich, Waverly has her favorite hairdresser, Mr. Rory, style her mother's hair. While Mr. Rory works, Waverly acts as though Lindo cannot understand English. Her anger flares when Mr. Rory points out how much Waverly looks like her mother. Looking at her daughter's face in the hairdresser's mirror, Lindo thinks about her girlhood, long ago in China.

On the eve of Lindo's tenth birthday, her mother told her fortune from her face. This incident happened before Lindo was separated from her mother and sent away to be married.

When Lindo was preparing to come to America, she paid money to a Chinese woman who had been raised in America and asked her to show her how to "blend in." The woman told Lindo how to answer common questions and then gave her a list of people to contact in San Francisco. For free, the woman advised Lindo to marry an American citizen and have children quickly. That would help her become an American citizen. Lindo wonders why Waverly distorts the facts of her past. Why does Waverly say that Lindo came over "on a slow boat from China" when she took an airplane? Why does Waverly say that Lindo met her husband in the Cathay House when it is not true at all? Lindo recounts the truth in a flashback.

When Lindo arrived in America, she sought out the people whom the Chinese woman had suggested. She found an inexpensive apartment. She also found a job—at a fortune cookie factory. There she met An-mei Hsu, who introduced her to her future husband, Tin Jong. At first, Lindo was appalled that he was Cantonese. But they struck up a friendship for they were both Chinese, despite the fact that they spoke different dialects. They communicated only in rudimentary English. An-mei convinced Lindo to use the fortunes from the cookies to communicate with Tin Jong. Lindo selected "A house is not a home when a spouse is not at home." She gave him the cookie, but he was confused by the word "spouse" and did not propose. The next day, however, he did and Lindo accepted. They were married the following month. Their first child was a son, whom Lindo named Winston. Vincent was born two years later, and Waverly after that. Lindo then turned sad; she became dissatisfied with her circumstances and hoped that Waverly would have a better life.

Back in the present, Lindo looks at her finished hairstyle. She sees how much she and Waverly look alike. Seeing her own broken nose, she imagines that Waverly's nose has been broken as well. Waverly brushes aside her Mother's observations with a laugh, saying that their noses are good because they look devious and two-faced.

Lindo recalls when she went back to China last year. Even though she took off her jewelry and wore Chinese clothing, people knew that she was foreign. She wonders what she has lost and what she has gotten in return.

In this story, we again see the themes of appearance and reality and the importance of heritage. To native-born Americans, both Waverly and Lindo appear to be "Chinese" at first glance. Mr. Rory, the hairdresser, assumes that Lindo cannot even speak English. Even Waverly plays into this misconception, treating her mother as though she were a recent immigrant. Lindo knows, however, because she is a citizen of China, that no one in China would ever mistake Waverly as a native Chinese; Waverly is unmistakably "American-made."

Lindo recalls how she tried to make Waverly both American and Chinese. She wanted her daughter to have the opportunities that America offered, yet still retain the obedience and wisdom of her Chinese heritage. She feels that she did not succeed; Waverly declares that she is "her own person." How could she be "her own person," Lindo wonders. She has not yet given her up.

Note the symbol of the crooked nose. Both Lindo and Waverly have crooked noses. Waverly is pleased with their noses, for she thinks it makes them look "devious" and "two-faced." Both of these words have negative connotations in English. Aware of these bad overtones, Lindo asks if it is a good thing. Waverly says that it is because "it helps you get what you want." This reveals Waverly's determination to succeed at any cost. Lindo is more subtle in her appraisal. She wonders how much of her is still Chinese, and how much of her has become American. Both women have a "double face," the title of this section, for they straddle two cultures.

The theme of heritage ties in with this duality. Waverly is unmistakably Lindo's daughter. In addition to appearance, they share many personality traits. Both are strong, focused women. The tie between them is undeniable. Recall how frightened Waverly was when she felt that it was time to tell her mother that she was going to marry again. She was unwilling to marry without her mother's approval. Lindo named her daughter "Waverly" after the street where they lived so that when the child grew up, she could "take a piece" of her mother with her.

This section is rich in humor and irony. It is ironic that for so many years Waverly denied her heritage. Now she is willing to embrace her culture because it is fashionable—but it is too late: Waverly knows only the most juvenile Chinese words and would never be mistaken for a Chinese person in her mother's birth country. An-mei's comments to Lindo are also ironically funny. "Did you ever think you would be so powerful that you could determine some one else's fortune?" she asks. This is ironic because the women cannot read—much less understand—the absurd fortunes that they stuff into cookies. Their fractured translations are as funny as the originals and make about as much sense to the two women raised on genuine aphorisms and wisdom. The entire situation in the fortune cookie factory is humorous, reminiscent of the famous *I Love Lucy* episode with Lucy and Ethel working on the chocolate assembly line. As with Lindo and An-mei, Lucy and Ethel work furiously to keep up with the output and are reduced to eating anything they cannot process. Recall how Lindo alludes to An-mei's round shape; she strongly suspects that An-mei eats the rejected cookies. Lindo's comment about subtracting some blessings for her broken nose is also humorous.

Note Tan's use of flashbacks. Like many of the other sections in the book, this one is constructed of a number of different flashbacks. This allows Tan to show how the past impinges on the present, how one's heritage flows through one's life like a river. Look through the sections to locate where the flashbacks begin and end. Find the "trigger words" that Tan uses to link the past to the present. Sometimes she leads directly into the section: "I am seeing myself and my mother, back in China, when I was a young girl." Other times, she uses memories and specific images.

Jing-Mei Woo: *A Pair of Tickets*

Jing-mei is on a train to China, traveling with her seventy-two-year-old father, Canning Woo. As the train enters Shenzhen, China, Jing-mei begins to "feel Chinese." Their first stop will be Guangzhou. Like her father, Jing-mei is weeping for joy. After her mother's death, a letter arrived from China from her mother's twin daughters from her first marriage. These were the two children whom she was forced to abandon on the side of the road in 1944.

Jing-mei's father asked Auntie Lindo to write back to the girls and tell them that their mother was dead. Instead, Auntie Lindo took the letter to the Joy Luck Club. Together, the women answered the letter, signing Suyuan Woo's name to it. Jing-mei agrees that she should be the one to tell her half-sisters about their mother's death. But after dreaming about the scene many times, she begs Auntie Lindo to write a letter to the sisters explaining that their mother is dead. Auntie Lindo does so.

The train pulls into the station, and the visitors are met by Canning's great-aunt. The reunion is emotional. Other relatives join them. Jing-mei wins her young cousin Lili over with instant photographs from her Polaroid camera. They soon arrive at a magnificent hotel, much grander than Jing-mei had expected. Jing-mei is anxious to have her first *real* Chinese feast; however, the native-born Chinese family decides that they want to eat American—hamburgers, French fries, and apple pie à la mode in the hotel room.

Late that night, Canning explains that his wife's name, "Suyuan," has two different meanings, depending on how it is written. Written one way, it means "Long-Cherished Wish"; written another way, it means "Long-Held Grudge." He further explains that Jing-mei's name means that she is first, a pure essence and second, that she is a younger sister. Her name makes her the essence of her two sisters. He then tells her the story of how her mother, Suyuan, abandoned Jing-mei's half-sisters.

Suyuan walked for three days, hoping to escape the Japanese invasion. Her hands began to bleed from the weight of her heavy possessions and that of her daughters. She dropped her possessions one by one, continuing to trudge on until she was delirious with pain and fever. She finally fell by the side of the road. Despite her entreaties, no one would take the babies.

Having no other choice, she stuffed jewelry under the shirt of one baby, money under the shirt of the other. Then she put in family pictures and a note and left her daughters to see if she could find food. Soon she fainted and awoke in the back of a truck filled with sick people who were being tended by American missionaries. When she arrived in Chungking, she learned that her husband was dead. She met Canning Woo in the hospital.

The abandoned babies were found by a kindly peasant couple, who raised the girls as their own. When the girls were eight years old, their foster parents tried to find their parents. They located the address of the children's home, but now it was a factory. Meanwhile, Suyuan and Canning had returned to try to find the girls, but their attempts proved fruitless. In 1949, they left for America, but Suyuan never abandoned hope. After she died, a schoolmate saw the twins in a department store and tried to contact Suyuan in America.

Jing-mei sees her sisters as she enters the terminal. At first, they look just like her mother. Later, she sees no trace of her mother—yet the women still look familiar. She sees in them the part of her that is Chinese. Her father takes a picture of the three girls; they look at the Polaroid photograph, and they see that together, they all look like their mother.

This highly emotional ending to the novel is based on a true incident from Tan's life. In 1987, Tan visited her half-sisters in China. At the time, her mother suffered from a dangerous heart condition and had recently suffered an attack of angina. Tan wanted to find out more about her heritage while her mother was still alive. The trip was a turning point in Tan's life. She explained her reaction in a July 4, 1989, interview in the *New York Times*. For the first time, Tan "felt a sense of completeness, like having a mother and a father," she said. "It was instant bonding," she continued. "There was something about this country that I belonged to. I found something about myself that I never knew was there." Her fictional creation, Jing-mei, shares the same reaction.

Through her meeting with her half-sisters, Jing-mei finds her heritage, her identity. At first, she is startled that her half-sisters look so much like her mother. Then she sees that there is no real resemblance at all. Finally, she realizes what makes them look so familiar lies beneath mere facial features. It lies deep in the blood. This theme reaches its climax in the final image of the book. It is only when the three sisters are together that they look like their mother. They share "her same eyes, her same mouth, open in surprise to see, at last, her long-cherished wish." Their mother's name—"Long-Cherished Wish"—has become truth.

This concept dovetails with the theme of appearance and reality, as well. The three sisters are their mother—and yet they are not. They look like her, yet they do not. Tan resolves the disparity by implying that there is no difference between appearance and reality: they are the same thing. Furthermore, such notions don't really matter; all that counts is the blood, the heritage. In effect, Jing-mei has bridged the generation gap.

Ironically, Jing-mei became like her mother long before she was aware of it. Like her mother, she was determined to get her money's worth. She was furious at what she perceives to be a mistake in their hotel booking. "I had explicitly instructed my travel agent to choose something inexpensive, in the thirty-to-forty-dollar range. I'm sure of this," she fumes. "Well, our travel agent had better be prepared to eat the extra, that's all I have to say." Her feelings match those of her mother when she had to deal with recalcitrant tenants or the local fish merchants. This characterization also serves to tie together the theme of transformations and the motif of the fairy tale.

Although the story of the half-sisters is based on truth, it has the ring of a fairy tale. Recall how Tan describes the twin babies as "little fairy queens waiting for their sedan to arrive." In keeping with this motif, the twins are left with jewels and money and possess a placid, regal nature. They sit quietly by the side of the road. As in a fairy tale, the princesses are taken in by honest peasants who raise them as their own children. The peasants see the girls as a sign of double good luck because they are twins. It's a classic fairy tale: the fairy queens left by the side of the road to be raised by poor peasants in a cave. The recognition scene also picks up on a fairy tale ending: like Cinderella, it involves shoes. Tan adds a contemporary twist that is a delicious bit of humor: the twins are shopping for shoes in a department store, not trying on shoes left behind at a ball, when they are discovered and recognized as being the daughters of the courageous Suyuan.

The structure of the ending unifies the book. Not only does this chapter pick up where the first chapter left off, but it also uses the same point of view and narrator. It continues the use of parallelism evident throughout the book, but most especially in "Feathers from a Thousand *Li* Away." Technical considerations aside, *The Joy Luck Club* is storytelling at its very best.

CRITICAL ESSAYS

Tan's Women

The novel traces the fate of four mothers—Suyuan Woo, An-mei Hsu, Lindo Jong, and Ying-ying St. Clair—and their four daughters—Jing-mei "June" Woo, Rose Hsu Jordan, Waverly Jong, and Lena St. Clair. All four mothers fled China in the 1940s and retain much of their heritage. All four daughters are very Americanized. As Tan remarked, the club's four older women represent "different aspects of my mother, but the book could be about any culture or generation and what is lost between them."

The four older women have experienced almost inconceivable horrors early in their lives. Suyuan Woo was forced to abandon her infant daughters in order to survive in a war-torn land; An-mei Hsu sees her mother commit suicide in order to enable her daughter to have a future. Lindo Jong is married at twelve to a child to whom she was betrothed in infancy; Ying-ying St. Clair was abandoned by her husband, had an abortion, and lived in great poverty for a decade. She then married a man whom she did not love, a man she could barely communicate with despite their years together.

By comparison, the four daughters have led relatively blessed lives, cosseted by their doting—if assertive—mothers. Ironically, each of the daughters has great difficulty achieving happiness. Waverly Jong divorces her first husband, and both Lena St. Clair and Rose Hsu Jordan are on the verge of splitting with their husbands. Lena is wretchedly unhappy and considering divorce; Rose's husband, Ted, has already served the divorce papers. Jing-mei has never married nor has she a lover. Furthermore, none of the daughters is entirely comfortable when dealing with the events of her life.

Although she has achieved great economic success as a tax account-ant, Waverly is afraid to tell her mother that she plans to remarry. Lena has a serious eating disorder, and she bitterly resents the way that she and her husband, Harold, split their finances, and how her career has suffered in order to advance his. Rose suffers a break-down when her husband moves out. She lacks self-esteem, and her mother cannot understand why she sobs to a psychiatrist rather than asserting herself. Jing-mei is easily intimidated, especially by her childhood friend Waverly. She is not satisfied with her job as an advertising copywriter and, like Rose, she lacks self-esteem.

Through the love of their mothers, each of these young women learns about her heritage and so is able to deal more effectively with her life.

The Fairy Tale

According to J.R.R. Tolkien, the "cauldron of story" has always been bubbling. Many stories persist in human memory, beginning long before the invention of printing and passed down through many generations to the present. This heritage, preserved chiefly through the "oral tradition," is the "soup" in the cauldron of Tol-kien's comparison—the ancient stories that have become part of all cultures. Yet, while making themselves welcome in different cul-tures, these stories have retained their core of individuality. The wide range of this literature has been divided into various cate-gories—myths, legends, fairy tales, folk tales, and fables.

Myths are generally about the creation of all things, the origin of evil, and the salvation of a person's soul. Legends, in contrast, are about the affairs of rulers and people in the eras before records were kept. Fairy tales, folk tales, and fables are about human behavior in a world of magic. Fairy tales are most often stories with an element of enchantment. Folk tales are short stories that have been passed down through word of mouth. As a result, folk tales include semi-historical accounts, legends connected with historical figures, and completely fanciful accounts of supernatural beings. The characters are often one-dimensional because the purpose of the folktale is to teach a moral. When an animal tale has a moral purpose, it is gener-ally called a fable. They often become part of legends.

As stories move from the ancient world to our own, they often undergo changes in style and purpose, blurring the distinction between the genres. While critics have spilled a lot of ink trying to make distinctions among these categories, most readers are more impressed by the ways that these stories are similar rather than different. First, everything is clear in a fairy tale or folktale. Readers can easily identify the hero and the villain. The evildoer is always punished; the good people are always rewarded.

Around the turn of the century, a number of authors began to blend the themes, plots, and motifs of folklore into their own storytelling. The most skillful of these writers never destroyed the basic strength of the folktale, but, rather, recreated the genre to forge a new creation. Some critics have dubbed this new creation a literary fairy tale, or art fairy tale. Chief among these writers are Hans Christian Andersen, Eleanor Farjeon, Carl Sandburg, Bernard Malamud, and Isaac Bashevis Singer. Amy Tan is working within this genre.

Modern Chinese History

China's history is both rich and turbulent. This is especially true in the twentieth century, a time marked by violent social, political, and economic upheaval in China. During the first decade of the century, Chinese students, merchants, and others who were dissatisfied with Manchu rule began to rebel. On February 12, 1912, the arch revolutionist Sun Yat-sen, who had been ruling as president from his quarters in Nanking, stepped down and, two days later, General Yuan Shih-k'ai was elected the first president of the Republic of China. In April, the government was transferred to Peking.

The Chinese Republic maintained a fragile hold on the country until 1949. Yuan died in 1916, and the provincial warlords governed the country for more than a decade, ever changing the political map of the country. During World War I, when Europe was absorbed with its own troubles, Japan sought to conquer China; in 1915, it issued the so-called "Twenty-one Demands,"which would have reduced China to a Japanese protectorate. China agreed to many of the demands, including the transfer of some land to Japan. China's belated entry into the war in 1917 was an attempt to check Japan's encroachment. Leaders fully expected America to support China against Japan, but they were mistaken. At Versailles, President Woodrow Wilson withheld America's support for China's restoration of autonomy because of 1917 agreements between Japan and the European allies and because Japan withdrew its demands for a racial-equality clause in the League of Nations. Chinese intellectuals were shocked by what they judged to be Wilson's betrayal. Increasingly, they turned to the ideals of the Soviet Union and communism—despite the fact that China was granted membership in the League of Nations.

The Chinese Communist Party was formed in 1921. Among its original members was Mao Zedong. Two years later, the Communists helped Sun Yat-sen reorganize the crumbling Kuomintang. In 1926, the strengthened Kuomintang, under the leadership of Chiang Kai-shek, tried to unify China under Kuomintang rule and rid the country of warlords and imperialists. Chiang purged the Communists and relied increasingly on foreign intervention. In 1928, he established a new government, but his rule was unstable. He failed to unify the country, and the Communists soon began to marshall the opposition. Mao Zedong rallied the peasants and set up opposition governments. Increasing Japanese aggression chipped away from the North and Manchuria.

On September 18, 1931, the Japanese exerted their control throughout Manchuria. The following spring they set up the puppet government of Manchukuo and installed Henry Pu-yi, the last of the Manchu dynasty, as its puppet ruler. The Communists continued to fight their way across the country on the so-called "Long March," and by 1936, they had established a strong base in the northwest. In 1937, the Kuomintang formed a united front with the Communists against the Japanese.

In 1937 Japan and China plunged into war. The following year, Japan seized control of most of northeast China, as far inland as Hankou, and the area around Canton on the southeast coast. World War II saw a serious erosion of power for the Kuomintang, while the Communists expanded their membership, military force, and territory. The Kuomintang was split into factions. Severe inflation, official corruption, and loss of morale further weakened the government. Meanwhile, the Communists continued to build strength.

On August 8, 1945, the USSR declared war on Japan and armed the Chinese communists. In 1945, shortly after Japan surrendered, tension between the Communists and Kuomintang erupted over Manchuria. The U.S. tried to mediate but failed. In 1949, the Communists seized control and established the People's Republic of China. Mao Zedong became the head of state and Chou En-Lai

(Zhou Enlai) seized the legislature. In 1954, Communism became law, and China began the transformation to a socialist society. Through extensive Marxist-Leninist propaganda, people were re-educated. Concubinage, polygamy, sale of children, and interference with the remarriage of widows was banned. Women were assured equal rights with respect to employment, property ownership, and divorce. Religion was controlled; missionaries were expelled. These changes were achieved through terror; between 1949 and 1952, more than two million "counterrevolutionaries" were executed.

Private industry was abolished and land reforms followed. Under the leadership of Chiang Kai-shek, the island of Taiwan off China's coast resisted Communist control and set up a rival government. In 1965, Chou En-Lai declared his intention to liberate Taiwan. The Communists sought to achieve their goal through air and naval raids but proved unsuccessful due largely to American intervention. Until the early 1970s, the U.S. supported the Nationalist government. In 1979, however, the U.S. began formal diplomatic relations with the People's Republic of China, ending its ties with Taiwan.

Rat	1936 1948 1960 1972 1984 1996	The rat's not a bad sign: you are brave, truthful, shy, smart, loving, and kind.
Ox	1937 1949 1961 1973 1985 1997	On the down side, you're a gossip and a tightwad. You're also charming, however, and hard working.
Tiger	1938 1950 1962 1974 1986 1998	You are a good student, a hard worker, intelligent. You are also impatient with those who do not measure up to the standards you set for yourself.
Rabbit	1939 1951 1963 1975 1987 1999	You are courageous. Kind to your friends, you are ruthless to your enemies.
Dragon	1928 1940 1952 1964 1976 1988	Westerners imagine dragons as fierce fire-eating monsters. The Chinese, in contrast, consider dragons as peaceful and kind. The dragon, in fact, is used in major Chinese festivals as a good luck symbol. The dragon sign is the luckiest of all. People born under the dragon are thought to be talented, trusted, and admired.
Snake	1929 1941 1953 1965 1977 1989	Energetic, healthy, and kind, you are also a real worrier.

Horse	1930 1942 1954 1966 1978 1990	You are lucky with money, smart, quiet, good looking, and a good dresser.
Sheep	1931 1943 1955 1967 1979 1991	You are well-liked, cheerful, intelligent but short-tempered.
Monkey	1932 1944 1956 1968 1980 1992	You are gloomy by nature but talented in art. You could make a lot of money with your talent.
Chicken	1933 1945 1957 1969 1981 1993	You are a genius, but very strong-willed and determined to get your own way.
Dog	1934 1946 1958 1970 1982 1994	You are a hard worker who keeps to yourself. You very much value your privacy. Also, you don't trust other people.
Boar	1935 1947 1959 1971 1983 1995	You are dutiful, loyal, and a leader. Unfortunately, you are also selfish and headstrong.

THE CHINESE LUNAR NEW YEAR

Birthdays are celebrated differently in China. A person's age is figured from the day of the Lunar New Year—not from the actual birth day. A child is one year old at birth and is two years old on the next New Year. Because the Chinese New Year replaces the birth day, it is a birthday festival for everyone, traditionally lasting fifteen days and ending with a Lantern Festival. Most businesses are closed for several days immediately following the New Year so that employees can enjoy the parades, which usually include a long papier-mâché dragon, concealing the long line of men who make it writhe and ripple.

No one knows for certain how long the Chinese have celebrated the Lunar New Year—the day of the second new moon after the winter solstice (a period between January 21 and February 19). Today, they use the Western, Gregorian, calendar—and have for over fifty years—yet they still observe their traditional New Year festivities.

The Chinese New Year is a time of mental, emotional, and literal housecleaning—the latter, to please the Kitchen God. One tosses out the old slate of mistakes and misgivings and begins a pristine, new slate. Fireworks displays are common during the period, as are feasts and banquets, and children receive gifts of money in small red envelopes. The traditional New Year greeting is *kung-hsi fa-ts-ai* (kung-she-fats-sigh), meaning "Greetings to you! May your year be filled with wealth!"

Each Chinese year is designated by one of the twelve animals of the Chinese zodiac. This symbol is especially helpful when one can't remember the year that a friend was born. If you recall that she was born in the Year of the Horse, for example, consult the following chart and you'll have a good chance of finding the year that your friend was born, as well as learning a few general details about her character.

REVIEW QUESTIONS AND ESSAY TOPICS

(1). Discuss the significance of the novel within the tradition of Chinese-American fiction.

(2). Analyze the conflicts between any two of these pairs of characters:
  • Suyuan Woo and Jing-mei Woo
  • An-mei Hsu and Rose Hsu Jordan
  • Lindo Jong and Waverly Jong
  • Ying-ying St. Clair and Lena St. Clair
  • Clifford St. Clair and Ying-ying St. Clair
  • Waverly Jong and Jing-mei Woo

(3). Compare and contrast the marriage of Rose Hsu Jordan and Ted Jordan to that of Lena St. Clair and Harold Livotny.

(4). Explain why the three remaining women in the Joy Luck Club contribute the money to send Jing-mei to China to meet her half-sisters.

(5). Discuss the function of the fairy tale in the novel.

(6). What is the significance of the story of the Moon Lady?

(7). What function do the four section openers, "Feathers from a Thousand *Li* Away," "The Twenty-Six Malignant Gates," "American Translation," and "Queen Mother of the Western Skies" serve?

(8). Who do you think is stronger—the older women in the book or the younger ones? Explain your answer.

(9). Show how two characters from the book search for a better life. Explain what each character tries to attain and the success of the quest.

(10). Discuss how *The Joy Luck Club* deals with the generation gap between mothers and daughters.

(11). Explain the theme of appearance and reality in the book.

(12). One critic has called *The Joy Luck Club* "intensely poetic." Isolate examples from the book to prove this assessment.

(13). Trace the autobiographical influences on the novel. What did Tan take from her own life and use in the book? How did she change these elements? To what purpose did she use them?

(14). *The Joy Luck Club* has been phenomenally successful, reaching the top of the best-seller list within months and garnering $1.2 million in paperback sales alone. Explain why the novel has been so well received by readers and critics alike.

(15). Which daughter in the book do you think is most like Amy Tan? Why?

(16). The novel has been called "rich in the bittersweet ambiguities of real life." Explain what the critic meant by this quote.

(17). Add another ending to the novel. Describe what you think happens to each of the four daughters and the three remaining mothers after Jing-mei returns home from China.

(18). Analyze the importance of food in the novel. What purpose does it fulfill? Which foods are most important and why?

(19). Compare the Chinese and Chinese-American cultures that Tan describes in this book to your own culture. How are they the same? How are they different?

(20). Explain how Tan uses symbolism in this book by analyzing at least three main symbols.

SELECTED BIBLIOGRAPHY

ANGIER, CAROLE. "*The Joy Luck Club*." (book review). vol. 95, *The New Statesman & Society*. June 30, 1989, 35.

AKER, JOHN. F. "Fresh Voices, New Audiences," *Publisher's Weekly."* August 9. 1993, 32-34.

_HAMBERS, VERNICA. "Surprised by Joy," *Premiere.* October 1993, 80-84.

CHATFIELD-TAYLOR, JOAN. "Cosmo Talks to Amy Tan: Dazzling New Literary Light." (interview). *Cosmopolitan.* vol. 207, November 1989, 178.

CHUA, C. L. "Review," *Magill's Literary Annual.* Englewood Cliffs, N.J.: Salem Press, 1992.

Contemporary Authors. Vol. 136. Detroit: Gale Research, 1993.

DONOVAN, MARY ANN. *"The Joy Luck Club."* (book review). vol. 163, *America.* November 17, 1990, 372.

"A Fiery Mother-Daughter Relationship," *USA Today.* October 5, 1993, D 12.

FELDMAN, GAYLE. "Spring's Five Fictional Encounters of the Chinese American Kind." *Publishers Weekly.* vol. 238, February 8, 1991, 25.

_____. *"The Joy Luck Club*: Chinese Magic, American Blessings and a Publishing Fairy Tale." *Publishers Weekly.* vol. 236, July 7, 1989, 24.

GATES, DAVID. *"The Joy Luck Club."* (book review). vol. 113, *Newsweek.* April 17, 1989, 68.

HUBBARD, KIM. *"The Joy Luck Club* has Brought Writer Amy Tan a Bit of Both." *People Weekly.* vol. 31, April 10, 1989, 149.

KOENIG, RHODA. *"The Joy Luck Club."* (book review). vol. 22, *New York.* March 20, 1989, 82.

LIPSON, EDNA ROSS. "The Wicked English-speaking Daughter." *The New York Times Book Review.* March 19, 1989, 3.

MASLIN, JANET. "Intimate Generational Lessons, Available to All," *New York Times*. September 8, 1993, C15.

MAYNARD, JOYCE. "*The Joy Luck Club*." (book review). vol. 95, *Mademoiselle*. July, 1989, 70.

MERINA, ANITA. "Joy, Luck, and Literature." (interview) *NEA Today*. vol. 10, October, 1991.

NEEDHAM, NANCY R. "By Their First Lines You Shall Know Them," *NEA Today*. May 1993, 27.

PATCHETT, ANN. "*The Joy Luck Club*." (book review). *Seventeen*. vol. 48, August 1989, 126.

PETER, NELSON, and PETER FREUNDLISH. "Women We Love: Nine Women Who Knock Us Out." *Esquire*. vol. 112, August 1989, 86.

SCHELL, ORVILLE. "*The Joy Luck Club*." (book review). vol. 46, *The New York Times Book Review*. March 19, 1989, 3.

SHAPIRO, LAURA. "From China, with Love," *Newsweek*, June 24, 1991, 63-65.

SKOW JOHN. "*The Joy Luck Club*." (book review). vol. 133, *Time*. March 27, 1989, 98.

"Tan, Amy." *Current Biography*. vol. 53, February 1992, 55.

YOUNG, PAMELA. "Mother with a Past: The Family Album Inspires a Gifted Writer." vol. 104, *MacLean's*. July 15, 1991, 47.